The White Girl

ALSO AVAILABLE BY DAWN KOSTELNIK:

The Adventures of the Audrey Eleanor (2014)

Current publications can be seen in:

The Northern Journal

The Yukon Times

The Whitehorse Star

THE WHITE GIRL

TRUE NORTH STORIES
BY DAWN KOSTELNIK

The White Girl

DAWN KOSTELNIK has 76 titles published on kobo.com

The author is currently working on a new novel, WOMAN WALKING. This will be a fictionalized storey based on fact. As a little girl of four winters, Mary, a First Nations Child walks through Mother summer and almost into Father winter from her far away birthplace in the Yukon Territory. Her parents now choose to live on the shores of one of Canada's grandest lakes, The Great Bear. Many winters later, her life trail is coming to an end; she has visions of her pathway to the stars, footsteps leading her to dance around the fire of the Borealis with her ancestors. Her eyes are old and weary from many trials, she stands with bowed head in Hiroshima Japan in 1998, the 50th Anniversary of the drop of the atomic bomb; she ponders her participation in this devastation, how will she face the old ones?

Typesetting: Massive Graphic, in Minion 10pt on 14
Cover design and layout: Massive Graphic massivegraphic.ca
Map: © Government of the Northwest Territories
ISBN 978-1-927812-98-3

I owe my life to my Paternal Grandparents
Vera Jeanette and John James Kostelnik; there can
never be enough thanks.

Preface

These stories as presented in separate chapters, previously made an individual appearance in the Whitehorse Star Newspaper in Whitehorse Yukon Territory Canada. The Whitehorse Star has served the Yukon and Alaska since its conception in 1900. In October 2013 re-runs of the White Girl began to make their weekly appearance in THE NORTHERN JOURNAL, norj.ca. On January 02, 2014 The Adventures of the Audrey Eleanor motored into the pages of the fledgling newspaper, The Yukon Times, yukontimes.com.

In June of 2008 the first of many, **ADVENTURES OF THE AUDREY ELEANOR** appeared in print in the Whitehorse Star. This one time adventure series turned into a bi-monthly full-page column that ran until its conclusion in December 2010. Cameo appearances popped up until May 2013, with fans demanding, "just one more Adventure, please". There are a few more in the queue that will be cast out to sea at a future date.

The Birth of the **WHITE GIRL** was on January 07, 2011 in the Whitehorse Star. The White Girl is True North Stories about growing up in the Arctic. These stories appeared as full page, bi-monthly columns as well. As individual units they are being published in a different format in the Northern Journal in Fort Smith, NT.

I have made the decision to publish each individual storey complete with my signature P.S. at the conclusion of each article as they were presented in the Whitehorse Star. Some of the meanings could be lost as local humour and dialect may be lost in translation. My hope is, that by leaving the stories 'as is' they provide the reader with real Northern Flavour so that the heartbeat of our song will pound in your veins.

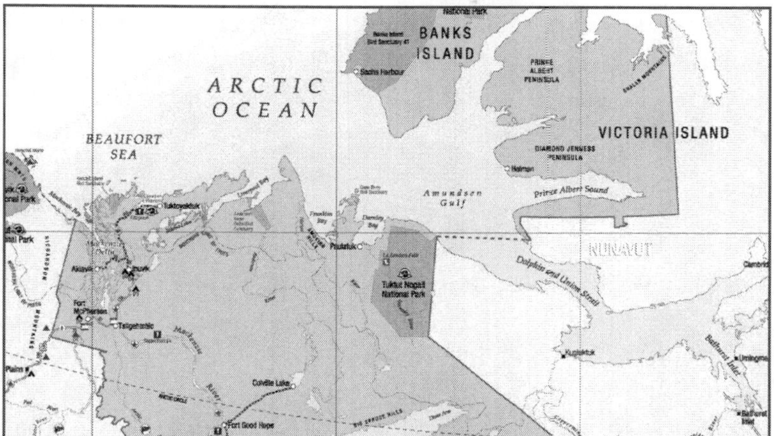

BANKS ISLAND
Sachs Harbour
ARCTIC OCEAN
BEAUFORT SEA
PRINCE ALBERT PENINSULA
VICTORIA ISLAND
DIAMOND JENNESS PENINSULA
Holman
Amundsen Gulf
Prince Albert Sound
NUNAVUT
Dolphin and Union Strait
Tuktoyaktuk
Paulatuk
Tuktut Nogait National Park
Aklavik
Inuvik
Fort McPherson
Tsiigehtchic
Kugluktuk
Colville Lake
Fort Good Hope
Great Bear Lake
Norman Wells
Deline
Tulita
MACKENZIE MOUNTAINS
YUKON
Elsa
Keno
Mayo
Crossing
Rae Lakes
Wekweeti
Wha Ti
Rae
Edzo
YELLOWKNIFE
Dettah
Lutselk'e
Wrigley
Fort Simpson
Jean Marie River
Fort Providence
Great Slave Lake
Fort Resolution
Hay River
Enterprise
Kakisa
Nahanni National Park Reserve
Nahanni Butte
Fort Liard
Trout Lake
Indian Cabins
Steen River
Wood Buffalo National Park
Fort Smith
Fitzgerald
Faro
Ross River
Johnsons Crossing
Teslin
Atlin
Upper Liard
Watson Lake
Lower Post
Cassiar
Liard River

Prologue

(BURIED ALIVE)

Lashing winds drive walls of snow across a vanishing trail. A single skidoo struggles to maintain its course on a track that is rapidly disappearing under the driven snow. The heavy skimmer bucks sideways in the drifts, pulling the skidoo with its human cargo off the track and into the deep snow. Skies are blackened, dusk combines with whiteout winds and shadows, there is no visibility.

The man and boy drop the heavy skimmer filled with mining equipment and try for the pass once again. They are doubled up on the old skidoo. Jane Creek Pass on the Old Dawson Trail shows herself seductively with glimpses to safety through the waves of snow and wind. If they can get over the pass, they can hide from the storm. Rick Cousins and his son Bobby are 65 Kilometres from Pelly Farm in the Yukon Territory, Canada. Bobby is twelve years old. They have 65 kilometres to go to hit their destination camp at Mariposa Creek; a consideration is Scroggy Creek, which is a closer 48 kilometres and offers possible shelter.

The strike of the early March storm in the Yukon is not unexpected, it is unappreciated. Weather is what defines us from outsiders, it just happens and we know it. Again they try to make the summit minus the skimmer, again they are swept backward, the return trail has already blown back in and drifted with swirling snow. The weight of two persons is too much on the skidoo, without a trail to follow it is impossible to reach the summit. Rick has a decision to make, a decision that no parent ever wants to have to make. He will have to leave his twelve-year-old son behind and break the trail ahead by himself.

There is no shelter from this storm. Rick digs a hole in the snow bank for Bobby. "I have to leave you here." He tells his young son. "I am going to bury you; this will keep you out of the wind and keep you from freezing until I get back." 'I have to do this, Bobby we won't make it over Jane Pass unless I break this trail." "We will die on this trail, do you understand?"

"Big brown eyes filled with trust look back at his father, "I believe we will die," he tells me later, but what he says to his father is," I know you'll come back for me."

“Listen for the skidoo,” Rick states, “I won’t be able to see you when I come back and I could drive over you.” “You will have to jump up and wave your arms when you hear me getting close.” “Don’t worry, you know I’d never leave you, I’ll be back.”

A young boy lays buried in a snow bank high on a mountain pass with the dark night galloping down the slopes. Wind howls and drives the snow hard on top of him. He lost the sound of his father hours ago it seems. He has no concept of time, he begins to worry. His mind is creeping into darker places than the approaching night. What happens if his dad gets lost or hurt climbing the mountain? Who would find him forty miles from anybody? It could be weeks until somebody even thought to look for him. Could he walk out without freezing to death? Not likely, there is food, an axe and matches on the skimmer, this gives him hope. If Dad doesn’t get back he will wait until the storm breaks and walk the distance back down into the trees to build shelter and light a fire.

He can’t remember if he brought his snowshoes along, it will be brutal wading through the snow if he forgot them. Will there be any type of trail to follow? Which way does he go? He hears something in the distance, is it real? He listens again, it could be a skidoo, the sound dies in the howl of the wind.

Again he hears it; he knows…his Dad is coming for him. His heart soars; he digs his way out of the snow bank and jumps in the air with arms waving. “Dad I’m here, over here!” A dim light from the skidoo heads toward him. Father and son hug each other hard. No time to waste, the winds have abated, they hitch up the skimmer and head quickly for the Pass. The trail once again is being lost to the wind and snow and dark. Over the Pass they creep, heavy with the weight of the skimmer. Falling black night decides the route, the trip is shortened they head instead for Scroggy Creek. On this wicked night, they are alive.

Bobby told me this storey a couple of years ago. I asked him if he told his friends about his adventures with his father. He said “no, they don’t believe me so I stopped talking about it.” It struck a chord with me, I said,” if you don’t tell someone these stories they will be lost forever.” He knew that, but did not know what to do about it. The extent of most of his friend’s adventures were done with video games on computers or movies on T.V. real life just couldn't be as exciting as that, could it? They didn't do this stuff, so how could he?

We have total empathy for John Firth and his skiing under the moose storey; it takes guts to tell these types of tales doesn't it John? It's appreciated.

I had stopped talking about growing up on the "river" years ago as well. I was sixteen when we moved to Whitehorse from Fort Smith NWT. My experience of attending F.H. Collins left everything to be desired. Living on the River I had acquired an accent with attitude. My father called it our Northern Accent. I was a sixteen-year-old white girl with an Old Crow Accent. Can you even imagine? Teenage white girls at FH Collins had a special brand of cruelty. The Vice Principal at the time called me into his office and suggested that I quit school. It was an excellent piece of advice. Since then I have told no one my stories, I am a White Indian, where do I belong? Who are my people?

What I learned when I was sixteen is that prejudice has little to do with skin colour it has to do with difference. For years I was the only white girl in different villages in the North. My friend Lolly said to me just a few years ago, "you were always heading up the hill, bleeding from some kinda hurt, snotty nose and crying frozen tears, somebody had pounded you out again." I was such a "mouthy thing" and just couldn't back down.

Insecurity and meanness can be cultivated in the hearts of all skin colours. When we teach it to our children it condemns them to the same hard life we say we want to avoid. When things are good, life is good, when things are bad people need someone to blame, pick the minority, whoever or whatever it is. In later years I knew it as the barnyard syndrome, this is where chickens will peck to death any other chicken that is a little "different". I learned that as long as we segregate rights to individuals rather than to the world as a community we create segregation.

Purple people demand different rights than the blue people, when we provide them with that right we SEPARATE, we create hard feelings. I have been a minority all of my life; I can feel a shift in the atmosphere and attitude of people; this is a good thing, this Age of Aquarius in our world, in our community.

It has taken four years of University English to smooth out my "accent". In a second it returns. Like a soft song, rounding off the syllables into slurs that could be a chant if you aren't listening close. It flows through my PC and into my stories. It's so easy to fall into the comfort of it rolling off of my tongue; my shoulders drop with the ease of usage.

The White Girl Series is an accumulation of events in my life as a little girl. I saw what will never be seen again, I have eaten food and lived a life that will not happen again. On one of our few ventures into the outside world my mother was asked to speak at the University of Alberta about our lives in the far North. We were living specimens of a lifestyle that no longer existed, even in the 1960's.

These stories are not what I've heard, these stories are what I've lived. The old legends I pass along were told to me directly by the Elders, who were alive at that time, some are stories specifically of them.

This series of stories has begun in Fort Norman, NWT now known as Tulita. They will continue on to include Fort Good Hope, Kugluktuk (Coppermine) on the coast of the Arctic Ocean and will conclude in Inuvik NWT. A second series is being considered, in which I will work my way south to Whitehorse. There are two sides to every storey and then there is mine.

P.S. The Captain and I are contemplating another type of water adventure. I am fortunate that Rick has worked in most of the communities that I grew up in; it gives him some insight into the cliffs that I walk off of during social functions. He has suggested that it is time to take a trip up the Mackenzie.

My friend Charlie Gaudet left this life a few weeks ago. His departure is significant in that he died of natural causes. A river of tears has already been shed for the lives lost due to suicide, drunk driving, stabbings and being fished out the Mackenzie with pants undone (impaired peeing). My age demands that I face mortality or at least face my friend's contribution to it. Without a doubt those of us that are left behind are amazed that we are here, payment is still due I suppose, spirits get stronger but flesh wears out. There are people that I need to see once more, it is time. I enjoy talking to you, your comments have been inspiring, mashi dwai.

Table of Contents

The White Girl

My name is Dawn Kostelnik and I am the White Girl, Mola 'tu 'we'/twa. In the 1960's my father was hired by the Canadian Government to work as an Indian Agent in the tiny native village of Fort Norman, N.W.T. My father is known by the people on the river as Somba ralla; the money-lender. My life is changed forever. The Dhe Cho becomes my home, the Mighty Mackenzie River in Canada's Arctic. This is the home of the Dene, a Native people of the River. I stand on the shores of a far away world and watch as civilization flies in politicians,whisky and toilet paper.

I am Mola 'tu 'we'/twa, the little white girl that bounces around the edges of the lives of ancient peoples. My ears are cocked for knowledge, my eyes wide open, my heart hoping that I will never forget these things that I have seen. Even as a very little girl I know that this way of life is slipping away. The old life is being carried up and far away to the stars with the winds created by the great new breath that heralds the arrival of the people of the south.

From the Mackenzie River I travel to the crystal waters of the Arctic Ocean. Home to smiling faces with almond eyes; their tongues mutter a language that catches in throats. Inuit, the eaters of raw meat, live in this vast frozen vista, witness to Islands that float high in the sky above rough diamonds of sea ice. Fermented seal flipper, indescribable. Old ways are remembered still, ancient beliefs lie embedded in the DNA of forgotten bones frozen in the permafrost; their wildness now running in the blood of the next generation of Inuktitut. (Eskimo). Come, listen.

Today I live in the land of gold, in Whitehorse, the capital city of the Yukon Territory, Canada. Whitehorse was once a city open and raw that well suited miners, pipeliners and trappers… and those with wildness in their hearts. Change is what happens, the politicians showed up here with the toilet paper and whiskey as well. They brought the bureaucrats from the south to fix what was not broken.

Where do those of us with the wildness in our hearts go? Is there a little piece of earth hidden behind the clouds and just over the mountain that still gives you room to breath and lets you live your life unshackled? I do not know this place today. I can only remember these places from when I was a child. Come with me and I will share these memories with you now.

These are my stories not to be confused with yours, some names have been changed some have not. Most of the people that I write about are still alive, if you think one of these stories is about you, it probably isn't. But let me know if it bothers you and I can change your name and take out your picture. This is not fiction.

P.S. May your heart be strong and the blood rushing through your veins be heated with wildness, may your spirit not be tamed and may you never become a sheeple.

In the language of the Northern Slavey, Mashi dwai/ Mashi Cho, thank you very much for travelling with me.

FORT NORMAN, N.W.T.

(Tulita)

... Is a tiny Native Village located on the intersection of the Bear River and the Mighty McKenzie River just 200 kilometers south of the Arctic Circle in Canada.

Most of the residents are Sahtu Dene and the language spoken is North Slavey and English. The population today is around 500 persons, at the time of these stories the population was about 300.

These stories are about real people in real times during the 1960's, I hope you enjoy them.

FORT NORMAN

THE BEGINNING
(NEW YEARS EVE 1965)

I am a little girl. My feet stick out in front of me on the worn green leather seat. Across from me on a duplicate seat that turns in to face mine, are my three younger brothers. I snuggle deeper into my fake fur coat. It is the most beautiful coat I have ever owned. It is blinding white in colour with a big shawl type collar that hides my nose if I want it to; my grandfather says that I look like a baby polar bear. It is a recent Christmas present from my grandparents.

It is very cold; we are between Christmas and New Year's sitting on the frozen tarmac at Edmonton's Municipal Airport. In the year 1965 it is early morning; the sun has lots of sleeping time left yet. A DC-6 airplane of the Pacific Western Airlines (PWA) vintage is struggling to warm up enough to start one last engine and get airborne in the minus -35F temperature. Northerners referred to PWA as the "please wait awhile" airline.

Windows on the old plane are mostly frozen over. My brothers and I have been blowing on the glass and scraping the frost away until our fingers burn with the cold. We stick them in our mouths and suck the frozen out. No one has stuck their tongue on the frozen steel that rings the window. This is luck only; knowledge is acquired harder, later.

The first engine has been rumbling for a time. With a struggle, the second engine coughs and spews diesel, possible rust particles and nuts and bolts onto the tarmac. Whatever it expels from its iron lung allows the engines to spark and they rattle into rotation. All engines are roaring and four wide-eyed kids tremble with anticipation, our first plane ride. We are not told to put on seat belts, there are none. No oxygen masks either. We lived through this, can you imagine? My nose is hidden in the white fur collar and I hug myself hard as the plane taxis down the runway. I don't know if I am afraid or so very excited.

Engine vibration bounces us around on the wide seats. We slide back into the worn leather as lift off carries us out and over the lights of downtown Edmonton. "Look, look," there are little dinky toy cars with headlights shining dimly far, far below us. Lights stretch out for miles into a dusky horizon; a drop in altitude drops my stomach as well. We are up in the air, we are flying, this is way better than the Ferris wheel. We have never been on a Ferris wheel, but we know that this just has to be way better.

Our destination on this trip is Fort Norman, N.W.T., it is now known as Tulita. Tulita was the long ago name that had been lost and now is found again. As a child I knew this village as Fort Norman and will call it that in my stories.

By way of tradition and age and the startling fact that I have lived this long, I am an Elder. These are stories of my life and are as I remember them. These are MY stories not to be confused with yours. You most certainly should write your own version.

My parents have researched Fort Norman, which is located on the Mighty Mackenzie River, the longest river in Canada winding and weaving for about 1,118 miles, in the then North West Territories of Canada. According to one encyclopedia, anything north of the Alberta border is a treeless wasteland that remains frozen solid for 10 months of the year. Peeping out the small hole that we have kept ice free we see miles and miles of green/black trees. Frozen white lines and circles define rivers and lakes and add patterns in the dark of the trees. This black and white vista continues on and over the horizon into infinity.

My mother is only 27 years old. Armed with this bit of miss-information, she flies into a vast unknown "wasteland" with my father, four small children and Sam the Siamese cat. Speaking plainly, my mother had guts.

Roaring engines initially deafen me, then slowly become a background hum. Our first stop will be Yellowknife, N.W.T. After refueling and loading cargo and passengers we will continue on to the "Wells" (Norman Wells), this DC-6 flies further north to serve the community of Inuvik as part of a scheduled service.

Yellowknife, N.W.T. we have landed. It is dusk or dark, the sun is off visiting someone, somewhere else. In the swarming snow everything shifts as shadows. People are dark shadows that move through softer grey shadows. We are hustled toward the terminal. Even in the few minutes it takes for this transfer, its' real apparent that my beautiful coat is not even close to being warm enough.

My feet are blocks of ice, created while sitting on the four-hour flight from Edmonton to Yellowknife. Clunk-clunk…eight little feet in frozen boots trudge across the snow swept tarmac towards the dim light of the terminal. People ask where we are going; eyebrows are raised in surprise at the response. We are an anachronism even in this era. White kids of school age were seldom seen heading into the high arctic, and never at this time of year.

I can hear the whispers; "they can't be taking that little girl in there – really!" For crying out loud even after the noise of the DC-6 engines I am not deaf! These people are scaring me and I have to pee. Is there a bathroom in this dark and noise? I am afraid to ask, I might have to go back outside and squat beside the plane. Someone on the plane said that the toilet was broken and we would have to pee in a jam can. I think I would prefer to squat by the plane. Such teasing, there is an inside bathroom at the airport and the one on the plane does work, these people are different, I don't know if they are making fun or not. I sure wish I had known that the toilet on the plane worked about an hour ago.

In this time Norman Wells is an oil town with a liquor store. Norman Wells was a camp that forgot to leave: I believe they were waiting for the Mackenzie Valley Pipeline. 20 years from now a pipeline is built to connect Norman Wells with Northern Alberta. The Canal Road connects the Yukon with Norman Wells.

Bunkhouses connected by boardwalks are my first memories of the "Wells". Howling winds swirl snow down the walkways and build banks in the corners of the metal ATCO trailer units, this was the Mackenzie Hotel. The bunk beds that are crammed into the tiny cubicles are made of metal as well.

With no T.V. and probably no radio, men would be jammed into these cubbyholes for endless nights during the long winters. How they maintained their sanity I don't know. Reading was an escape, as well as card games that would continue after shift work was completed. Some card games carried on for days.

My mom throws back the bedding to inspect the beds before we are allowed to crawl in with our clothes still on. The inspection of one bed elicits a half-scream from her; I don't know what she found, she never said and I don't want to know. Bare light bulbs protrude from the wall above the pillows on the bunks. We are a few hours into dream land when billowing toxic fumes interrupt sweet dreams of sugar plums from Christmas just past.

Portable trailer units will flare and consume their contents in minutes. My brother Joel's pillow has caught on fire. His pillow was pushed up against the bare light bulb; it smoldered and finally burst into flame. The fiery pillow is beat out against the floor but the noxious fumes remain. It is too cold outside to open the door of this tin can to air out the room, we have to cough ourselves to sleep with smells of burnt feathers and electrical wiring.

Once day breaks with just enough light to fly, we climb aboard the Beaver airplane that will take us the remainder of our trip into Fort Norman. My cat Sam has to stay behind for a few days, we are so over loaded that his slight poundage and the tiny bit of space he takes is too much. He can't come with us, he will be sent in on the next scheduled flight. He is an unusual visitor and will be thoroughly enjoyed by his babysitters; cats do not survive long in this land of sled dogs. It is less than an hour flight with the Beaver into Fort Norman.

My mom sits up front with the Pilot; this is his first trip into Fort Norman. Dad is stuffed into the back with four wide-eyed and frozen kids. Bear Rock is a "mountain" located at the confluence of Dhe Cho (the Mackenzie River) and Sahtu Dhe (the Bear River). It is a sacred mountain, which is the home of the legend of Yamoria. A monument that announces you will be landing in the village of Fort Norman within minutes. It is also an area of great wind shears. Senior Pilots know to give Bear Rock a wide berth; our pilot is new, he is not aware of this danger.

In front of us is the mountain, the sinewy fingers of the Giant Beavers of Yamoria fame clench suddenly over our plane and hurl us toward the ragged river ice. Our plane plunges and dives toward a cruel and sudden death on the mighty Mackenzie River. Engine screaming, my mom is screaming, I can't hear her, her mouth is open in terror but I can only hear the screaming of the plane engine as we plummet.

My mom is beside the pilot and has a front row seat as our plane is driven hard toward jagged ice. We are pushed into each other and lumped up against the back of her seat and the pilots. I look away from her and can see nothing through the windshield but huge shards of ice and hard packed snow, point zero is coming up fast!

Suddenly our pilot takes command of his plane, with a roar the nose of the plane is righted! In a drama that only real life can present we are hurtling skyward in our little rocket ship, wings tipping wildly our pilot fights to control our tiny plane. A few more seconds and we would have been dashed into bits of raven bait on the frozen Mackenzie.

"Wow, what a ride, that was pretty crazy!" My mom's face matches the white of the snow. We will re-live this adventure for days to come; I maintain a fear of flying to this day. "Did you feel your tummy come into your mouth?" "We were gonna smash into the ice!" "Our guts would be everywhere!" "Do you think it would hurt when we crashed down?" I am glad that we won't be flying outside for awhile.

A bombardier arrives to pick us up at the 'airport' in Fort Norman. The airport is a simple gravel and snow runway with no outbuildings. It is cleared when needed by an old D-4 cat. Bart Hawkins is a member of the welcoming committee; I think he must be a giant. He is bundled up in traditional RCMP winter garb; his fur hat completes the picture. With a huge smile he welcomes us to Fort Norman. He picks me up like I am a feather and puts me inside of this dark metal box that runs on tracks over the snow.

The future Chief of Fort Norman, Paul Baton ushers my brothers in, in much the same way. Kurtis, the baby is handed to me for safekeeping, I am his seatbelt. With a wild lurch the tracks break free of the snow they have already frozen to and we are off. Swaying and jerking we climb snow banks and drop into gullies. Our breath freezes and creates a cloud inside of this ponderous tank, talk is limited. All concentration is used to maintain our position on the frozen benches that run along the sides of the bombardier, it is so very, very cold!

There will be a dance to bring in the New Year! I love to dance, my grandfather taught me how to waltz by standing on his shoes. I wonder what kind of music they will play here? We are all going to the community hall for this dance. The community hall is a log structure at the bottom of the hill past the McPhersons and Douglass houses. There are no street names.

It is dark; it seems to be dark all of the time. My family is assembled on the front steps of the log hall. This is not a very big building, maybe 30 feet by 40 feet. Smoke and sparks from a wood fire pour out of the chimney into the star sprinkled night sky above us. How can they fit a whole town in here? It is best for us to enter all at once; we don't want to let the heat inside escape.

A blast of cold air presented in a cloud of frozen condensation announces our arrival to everyone on the inside. Two 45-gallon fuel tanks have been converted into a double burning wood stove, one on top of the other; they are glowing red in the dim light of the entry. A smokey haze layers the room, a combination of cigarettes and wood smoke. Rifles propped up along the back wall of the wood stoves keep them out of the way and prevent them from freezing up. Wolves and packs of dogs are real threats on the dark trails that lead back to homes.

People are coming to meet my parents. I am having a hard time understanding what they are saying. They speak words that sound like English, but with another language underneath. Their words are soft, like singing a song. Brown hands pat my very white fake fur coat. I can see feet and more feet in beautiful hide shoes. Furs of all type trim out mukluks and parkas and vests. Flashes of brilliance sparkle off of beads that glitter on clothing as everyone moves around visiting with neighbours. Leather clothes smell like the wood stove but better.

A pulse has started to beat in the next room. The beautiful shoes slowly begin to shuffle in time to the pulse. What is this sound? I see a doorway that leads into a darker room yet. The pulse is stronger, glints of colour from the beads on the beautiful shoes have found life, they flash and glitter as the shoes set definite steps in time to the throbbing beat.

Stronger and stronger, I can feel the beat of my heart; this sound is the beat of my heart! Rhythmic and strong my body has adjusted my heartbeat to pound with this pulse that is pulling the people. Chanting starts and a human chain forms. A man has to lead the dance; women fall in and kids tumble about. Feet hammer on the springy wooden floor; a hundred hearts beat in unison. I want to do this, can I do this, will they let this white girl dance?

My decision is made for me as my arm is taken and I am pulled into the living chain. Cautiously my feet shuffle, and then stamp with the beat of the drums. We are part of a single heartbeat; we are all part of the drums. Chanting hits crescendos that cause my skin to ripple with goose bumps and separate from my body, my hair is standing straight up. In this dark and smokey room, we are following the most ancient rhythm of life, the beating of a heart; the floor bounces in rhythm beneath us.

Darker faces in a dark room pounding with drums and song. In this pulsating mass of humanity there is a white fake fur coat that stands out like a full moon on a blue night.

This is the White Girl.

FORT NORMAN

INDIAN AGENT

My father is Somba ralla. Translated from Northern Slavey this means he is the moneylender to the people of the Sahtu Region on the Mackenzie River in the NWT, known as Fort Norman. He is John Kostelnik the Indian Agent to the white people. The people on the river like him. There is no honour in pretending to like someone when you don't. Men come up and say "John, how are ya" doin'?" "What we doin' today?" Their smiles shine through their eyes; my father makes things happen, they know he is a good man. It makes life easier for me because the people like my dad.

My father has been hired to do this job by the Federal Government of Canada. Since we have moved to Fort Norman a new entity of power has come into being, the brand new Territorial Government. The Territorial Government will now act as the governing agent for the Northwest Territories.

A new word creeps into the language of government, "Self Government". Self- Government for whom? Taking baby steps, the Territorial Government begins to deal with governing the people of the Northwest Territories. When a governing force does not live where they govern, concerns of their constituents cannot be fully addressed. How can someone in Ottawa relate to a village that has no water or sewer system, no telecommunications, no roads? Really, it is difficult to understand what you do not know.

A suggestion of self-government for the Indian Bands is also being carried on the winds. We live in incredible times. My father would remain with the title of Indian Agent until his term in Fort Norman ended. Indian Agents would be no more, their title changes to Area Administrators. My father is the last person on the Mackenzie River to maintain the title of Indian Agent. There is a good possibility that he was the last person in Canada with that designation as well.

As the Indian Agent it is his job to drum up work for local people, dis-

Irene Baton, Dawn and Joel Kostelnik

tribute assistance money, convince the government that new out houses were not a luxury and yes people would appreciate having power in their houses. When it was called for he was the coroner and arranged to bury the dead. He was the mayor, local contractor, mechanic, fisherman and hunter, digger of holes…he did not have to do all of these things, but he did. People could tell that he cared, they talk of him still and he remembers them well.

Jingle, jingle the sound of sleigh bells tinkles in my ears. A dog's face breaches the crest of Douglass's hill. He is the lead dog, his head is low to the frozen white road, he pants out hard frosted puffs. Behind the lead dog four more sled dogs are digging in to drag the carryall with its load of firewood to the top of the hill. Their master is running somewhere below the sleigh. The dogs are strong but the weight of the man would wear them out before they got home with the firewood. He runs behind his team and yells directions, "gee, gee…."

Standing politely by the side of the road I watch as they get closer, this is my first close up look at a dog team. Smash! I can't breathe! I am squashed by a huge weight on top of me. Gasping for air the blue, blue sky fades in and out. It is my frozen breath and someone else's that is clouding my vision. I'm going from scared to mad in short order, someone has thrown me off of the road and jumped on me, what the hell?

'Moola ya (white man's kid) are you crazy?' 'Them dogs gunna' chew you up.' 'Them bells means get the hell off the road, them dogs will eat you.' 'You better smarten up Moola ya, you won't make it!' A boy not a lot older than I am is yelling these words of wisdom in my face. He is reacting with fear for me, I haven't settled down enough to realize this; I'm just thinking that he's a meanie and I'm revving up into full blown mad!

Patiently he explains that anytime a dog team is going through town they are supposed to wear bells. This warns people that they are coming and gives them time to get right out of the way. This does not mean standing on the road, this means running for the ditch and jumping into the deep snow. These dogs will attack and will kill.

There are no modern day illusions that their wild has been bred out of them and isn't sitting seconds below the surface. The people here know better. Sometimes he says, people don't put bells on, you have to listen for the sound of the sled or the master (they were not called mushers) yelling gee or haw for the lead dog to head left or right, some guys just point the way they want their dogs to go, you need to LISTEN and pay attention if you want to live.

His name is Alvin, he becomes my friend. He was my teacher in those first days. 'No, no don't talk to those big kids like that, they will pound on you.' 'Don't even look at them, they will think you're a smartie or a proudie and will really pound on you.' 'Don't walk across open fields, dogs might be buried under the snow on the chain line you won't see them until they jump on you.' 'Look for dog chains around houses before you go up to the door.' 'Deh (come) and quit asking so much questions or I won't take you sliding on Father's hill.' 'I'll teach you swear words in Slavey, I'll teach you Slavey so you know what the big kids are saying so you can run.' 'You're too little to fight.'

Porridge arrives in school after singing Oh Canada to the Canadian Red Ensign with the Union Jack Flag (no one had bothered to replace it with the Maple Leaf yet), then we say the Our Father, this is a Catholic School, a Catholic community. We get fed porridge and vitaminized biscuits, these we call dog biscuits because we are pretty sure that if there ever could be such a foolish thing they would taste like this. Can you ever imagine making cookies for dogs? Such a thing! Chocolate covered, liquid centered vitamins were so good that you could use them to trade for bread.

On exceptional days we have caribou soup and homemade bread that Fred Gaudet makes. This is my favourite it is so good. Mr. Gaudet blinks his eyes in amazement when the little White Girl asks him for his recipe. "I just throw stuff in the pot!" I am patient, I ask "how much stuff?" He shakes his head and walks away. He is not used to talking to little girls. Later he comes up to me and bends over, "caribou parts, a can of tomatoes and macaroni, other days it's what we got hanging around." He turns on his heel and walks away. So now I know.

Once a week our heads are inspected and combed through with a lice comb looking for nits. If the comb didn't come back with bugs and eggs you went into the shower. If the little critters were discovered, the comb was dipped in kerosene and run back through your hair, you sat for a few minutes, then you went into the shower. This was an individual shower, in order to get the whole class smelling of sunlight bar soap it took a full day. Cases of lice weren't as prevalent as I hear parents complaining about today. Before you wonder at the use of kerosene for de-lousing check the ingredients of the stuff you use today on your kids heads that doesn't work.

My classroom held grades beginner to grade two. The classroom next door went from grades three to five or six. After that you went to residential school in Inuvik, Yellowknife or Fort Smith. Usually white families that ventured north in those years either didn't have kids or made sure that they left before their kids were of school age. We were not usual. My brother Joel was in grade one, I was in grade two.

I love my teacher, Miss Web, she is very gentle and kind to the little kids and she likes to do artwork. Grade beginners were primarily an English class for the tiny kids. English was spoken at school, Slavey was spoken at home. Playing with the other kids, they spoke English until it got easier to speak Slavey. Swearing was done in Slavey cause we were Catholics. Ours was a collaborative language with broken English and combinations of river Slavey, which changed depending on the community a person came from, we knew what we were talking about.

The church basement was our best playground when it was -40f. Father Labatte, our priest was the biggest of all the kids. He made stilts out of almost anything; we all had a pair that he made for us. Dancing up the church steps on his stilts was something that he did to make us laugh. In the basement we played soccer and every ball game he could think up.

On warmer days he drilled cross-country skiing into our bodies and pounded it into our brains. This was the almost era of Sharon and Shirley Firth and Freddie Kelly, known as the Kelly Express. Freddie was from Fort Good Hope just a day away by boat north on the Mackenzie River. I do believe that at night the priests got on their VHF radios and compared notes with Father Mouchet in Old Crow as to who were their most promising skiers and what their best time runs of the day were. We had Ernie Lennie to compete with. He set the bar for us kids.

In 1969 Ernie Lennie placed in the Canadian Junior Championships and went on to compete in the 1976 Olympics in Montreal. He skied in competitions in Russia and Austria; he left big skis for us little kids to fill. Father Labatt was determined that one of us would fill those skis. In the summer he tried to keep us busy picking potatoes. It always started out great, then the first potato got thrown, then the second and in the flash that his back was turned it was potato wars. He would make us pick gooseberries for penance.

Father Labatt would answer the phone at the rectory," good day Labatt's Brewery." It was rumoured that when the bishop of the day called and received this salutation he didn't see the humour in it. Father Dene' replaced Father Labatt.

Father Dene was a quiet gentle man who brought in classic comics for us to read. I read and re-read everything from Treasure Island to Hound of the Baskervilles in comic book form at least a hundred times. We did not have television or a library, I even read schoolbooks on Canadian History, my appetite for books is insatiable.

At the church we are standing on the steps deciding what we could do next for entertainment. We had just re-read the comics and didn't feel like sliding on Fathers hill. Suddenly my brother Joel sticks out his tongue and licks the steel handrail. It is a full on lick. Eyes are open wide in astonishment, wow that takes guts, or did he just go crazy? His tongue will not come off intact.

Father Dene comes out of the church to see what the commotion is, Phoebe Gaudet is with him. Mrs. Gaudet (she is Fred Gaudets's sister-in-law) turns in an instant and heads back inside the rectory. My brother is now in terrible pain. Even amongst a group of really tough kids, there is only sympathy. Eddy says that he always wanted to try that. We watch in silence, our faces contorting in empathy for him.

Mrs. Gaudet returns on a run with the kettle of hot water. Joel's tongue is a combination of frozen and boiled meat, but he is loose! He is tough; he has to paint his tongue with purple medicine for a week. His teeth are purple too, he is our hero, "show us your tongue, show us your tongue!"

It's kinda' hard to see where the skin has been torn off his tongue cause of the purple colour, but we get the idea. Father Dene always had an extra kind word for Joel after he left his tongue skin on the church rail.

P.S. Did you know that there is no sweat in the Arctic eh! Talk to you after a while, Mashi Cho.

FORT NORMAN

HUNTING REALITY

One hundred and twenty six dogs stretch out across the frozen Mackenzie River. Eighteen teams of dogs become thin lines of broken black thread that sew their way toward the even blacker ridge of pecker pole pine and spruce that frame out the western shore of the mighty Mackenzie. This is the western side of the NWT that borders with the Yukon Territory.

It is time for the early spring hunt. The men will be gone until they have killed enough caribou to feed us through to the last part of March and until the ice breaks up. Then everyone heads for fish camp and rat camp. A rag tag group of kids watches in silence as our fathers, uncles and brothers head out to hunt food for us.

John Kostelnik with his 'Old Boys' the team of Freighter Dogs rescued from Fort Smith. They are heading out across the Mackenzie for a hunting trip in 1966.

We stand silent on the bank, eyes straining for the last glimpse of men and dogs as our village is emptied. Little arms wave, just one more time… our dads disappear into the distance and dark of the trees. Cold forces us to finally leave the riverbank. Women and children and old men are left to manage until the food comes home again with the men and dogs. The Ehtee (grandfathers) have to keep us safe from the wolves.

My dad has his own team of dogs, his boys. They are "end of their day" dogs that were going to be shot at the end of their working days. My dad brought them home to us instead. Food is used for usefulness, there is no free ride, and there are no pet dogs. These are ex-freighter dogs from Wood Buffalo National Park in Fort Smith NWT. They have been the Superintendents dogs and he is happy not to have to shoot them. My dad is happy to have his own team.

The freighter dogs are gentle giants. Dogs with heads like grizzly bears, especially "Smiley". Scars cover Smiley's head from dogfights, ears bit off, white-faced old man, he always smiles at us kids, lowering his head in submission for an ear scratch. Whitie is my dog, he is our lead dog. He has the presence of a wise old man, calm and always watching. Sam and Roy conclude the team of imported four.

A wheel dog has the toughest job, they are the dog harnessed closest to the sleigh, they have to pull hardest. Tippy our wheel dog is of a different ancestral destination, he is local talent. He is a black and white, blue-eyed Siberian husky, smarter than most with a hatred for other dogs that becomes legend.

Physically these freighter dogs are almost twice the size of the local dogs weighing in at 125 lbs. These dogs are twice as slow as the local teams; my dad always comes home last. They can pull double the weight of the other dogs, but they are old guys and so compensation has to be made for them. They are the perfect "starter" team. Whitie will stop if dad falls off of the sleigh; most dogs just keep on going, looking over their shoulders laughing as they run off down the trail.

Our dogs sit patiently and wait for dad to put on their tracers and stand when he needs to secure straps and buckles. They teach my dad lots about running dogs. (I never heard the term mushing until we moved south to Whitehorse)

A grub box includes a small bag of flour, baking powder, salt, lard, sugar and tea. A little dry meat is stashed out of sight if someone is lucky enough to still have any left from the fall time. Women make small bannocks that will carry the men for a few days. Bales of dried fish are packed for the dogs; the men can eat this as well. The weight of the sled has to be kept down, gear is minimal.

Tents, tea pails and cast frying pans are shared, there are no suitcases, an extra pair of socks is acceptable. Tobacco and snoose (snuff) is a luxury that will run out before the hunt is over; little pinches of snooze are shared around the fire at night.

On this hunting trip they are headed towards the Plains of Abraham that have been a hunting destination for Deh Cho people as well as the Ross River people. MacMillan Pass is beyond the plains. In a straight line it would be about 350 miles to Ross River from Fort Norman. The hunters are not looking for Ross River, YT; they are locking for the closest herd of caribou.

Travelling great distances requires great amounts of food and energy. There is danger in this equation, the chances of men and dogs getting hurt increases by days on the trail. On a regular hunting trail you come across snares that have been set by other hunters, this was not a regular route for the hunters, there are no pre-set snares. A frozen rabbit could be pulled out and the snare was reset for the next person. There is no room for error on this trip; they have to find meat fast. One hundred and twenty six dogs and eighteen men need a lot of food to survive and return home to their families.

Thousands of caribou blacken the plains; the men have been breaking trail for two days. Cold has bitten fingers and toes, my dad is losing weight, and he has none to lose. Miles of trail has been broken with snowshoes; this trail ends at this herd. Dogs are jumping in their tracers; men with weary arms struggle to hold the dogs back.

This herd is massive; it will take time for thousands of caribou to pass. Even with the spur of howling and barking dogs. Breath, frozen with cold fills the air as the struggle to maintain control of the dogs continues, the caribou are making their own cloud of fog. Skies are a brilliant blue in the background; treetops are packed thick with snow. Trees deceptively short, poke four feet of their tops in the air, the balance of them buried in twenty feet of snow.

Rifle shots begin to reverberate off of mountaintops. Echoes ricochet from exposed rock faces; avalanche conditions are prime, but forgotten in the focus of the hunt. This herd continues on its genetic trek, its size dictates that it will reach its destination despite this bite from the hunters. As the herd swerves around shot and dropped bodies that create islands in the snow, the men continue to fire, picking out choice animals.

In the end, 160 caribou are shot and the work begins. One hundred and sixty caribou have to be gutted and piled. Livers from the caribou are thrown in the frying pan as they are taken, or eaten warm and raw. They will not have to haul the meat home; the luxury of having an Otter fly in to pick up the meat has been prearranged. The payment for this "luxury" is that they have to pack an airstrip with their snowshoes for the plane to land on.

For two more days the men take turns trying to pack down "sugar" snow with their snowshoes. The airplane won't arrive until they return to the village to make a radio call, instructing the pilot to fly out for the caribou meat. Six caribou a night are needed to feed the hunters and dogs.

One hundred and sixty caribou piled one on the other creates a small meat mountain. Tents are used to cover the frozen flesh while the hunters' head for home. The hunters will now be sleeping in the open by the fire; it is still -35 f at night. Spruce bows are cut and woven into a platform for sleeping and sitting. Caribou ribs are hung over the fire by a three-poled tri-pod to cook and get slightly smoked, my goodness they are good. Tea is thick and black sweetened with sugar and flavoured with spruce needles, the best.

A blizzard blows in on the second day towards home. George Pelletier's dogs surprise a moose on the trail. A snarling tangle of dogs taking on a Bull Moose is destructive. Yelping dogs are thrashed by slashing hooves, thank god the moose has lost his antlers; George can't get to his gun, it's in the carryall under the dogs and angry moose. He turns and runs back down the trail through the sheeting snow searching for another gun. Everyone has their brake on and are waiting…howling winds carry tattered sounds of snarling yelping dogs, are there men's cries as well?

Nothing, nothing, George comes on my dad first; dad hands him his rifle and watches as he disappears back into the blowing snow. Bang, bang…the rifle is muffled in the windstorm. George will have to snowshoe home if the moose kills his dogs. Limping but intact, the dogs will carry George and parts of the moose towards home.

A shout goes up in the village, a drum sounds at the far end of town. Hunters are coming, hunters are coming. The heartbeat of the drum calls us to the river bank, look, look there they are, they are coming, hurry, hurry…kids empty out of the village, we are all running down the river bank, out onto the ice.

Haggard dogs and men get closer and closer, some men are riding inside the carryalls, dogs run with long tongues, grabbing bits of snow for thirst. We don't care how tired they are we are looking for our dad's. Kids jump into the sleighs and on top of our fathers, uncles get teased as we run along side of them looking for someone else, the dogs are too tired to bite even. They are home, they are home. Inside the carryalls is a little fresh meat for tonight. We will dance to the drums and eat moose drizzled with lard.

P.S. this was a communal hunt; the Chief George Horsey distributed the meat every Saturday to the people. It took three trips for the Otter to bring the meat into Fort Norman; this food carried us through to break up. In the two weeks this trip took, my Dad lost 10 pounds of weight, he says that he ate as much as he could; there is no fat on winter caribou. Running behind a team of dogs that are weighted down makes you skinny. In order not to starve, he began to mix the dogs oatmeal into his tea for some carbohydrate.

FORT NORMAN

BREAK UP OR BOMBS?

There has not been a plane in weeks. It is break up in the Arctic. This is 1966 in Fort Norman on Deh Cho, the MacKenzie River in the NWT, Canada. I am a little girl sitting on the banks of this mighty river with every other kid in town. Our ears strain for the sounds of cracking ice that will indicate the mile wide band of solid water in front of us will break up and free us from this prison!

Small bush planes provide us with mail and the occasion movie reel in big cans; we have been watching "The Vikings" a movie starring Kirk Douglas, Tony Curtis and Ernest Borgnine for the past month. With not much else to do we re-enact this movie everyday at recess and after school. With wild shouts to Odin, a Viking god of some sort we engage in battle. We have all suffered wounds dealt by blows with wooden swords and willow spears made especially for this, no one has lost an eye…yet.

Kids head home everyday with snotty noses from crying and bloody noses from hard contact, me included. This particular program is getting old, even for us. The snow is too soft to ski and the ice on the river is rotten or candle ice so we can't cross the powerful MacKenzie River to set snares, we are caged tigers. We need a different movie!

Our teachers are "bushed", a northern term for the mental hangover of a long, dark and hard winter. Our principle is acting strangely. He has locked the door to our classroom several times to try to upset our teacher. It works; she yells at him, we watch this hiding behind our books. When you hide behind your book nobody can see you do anything! If

Back left row is Irene Baton. Front left is Dawn Kostelnik, Sarah Gaudet, Eddy MacPherson, Alvin Yallee

he doesn't let us out we can't go to the bathroom, the little kids will pee their pants.

He's getting pretty goofy. Today they are sword fighting with yard-sticks; maybe they have been watching our schoolyard performances. The use of yard sticks puts them in a category well below what we use, babies compared to us. Poof, clouds of chalk dust billow into the air, they are throwing chalk brushes at each other and keep missing. It is hard not to laugh and giggles are breaking out and interrupting the performance. Our teachers realize how silly they are, they look at each other sheepishly. Break up needs to come soon, the principle returns to his class.

Spring break up is a time of reclamation. Days are longer; if you put your back to a wall and stand still you can squeeze some warm out of the sun. Sol, the passive aggressive orb in the sky smiles as it melts away the hard cold. Faces tan from sun glancing off the snow and ice. Little rivets of water are running down the road and dropping like tiny waterfalls from roofs. Bird song is heard in the willows. People who have the "sight" can see sap running in the trees and willows.

There are strangers sitting on porches and steps, they have not been seen for months. Elders have left the warmth of the woodstoves to creep outside to bask in the warmth and light of the sun for a few minutes. Cold sneaks quickly into old bones, they sigh as they are forced, reluctantly, back into the dark and fetid cabins.

Ice is rotten and unpredictable, snow gets sticky and sleds suck into slush that refuses to let go. The winter weary dogs stumble at their task. These dogs have hauled wood all winter to keep their masters warm; in the summer they rest. Their tired eyes say that it can't be soon enough. We have no cars or trucks to haul people or wood. Dogs are skinny from hard work; their rib bones stick out and rub the tracers that attach them to the sleigh. Caribou meat and stick fish ran out a month back and masters are cooking what they can for their dogs.

Commercial dog food is an inferior product, it runs right through a dogs guts. Caribou or moose hair is added to the cooked commercial feed. Hair holds the food in their gut longer in an attempt to let the dogs pull some nutrition out of this stinky mush; some are lucky enough to have tallow and oats to add to the cooked feed, at the very least, it's warm. People are hungry too, there is little food left at the HBC.

The White Girl in the foreground. In the background to the right is Sarah Gaudet in the middle Raymond Yakeleya, on the left Charlie Gaudet, July 1st, 1966, Parade in Fort Norman

White men in suits with really white shirts came from Ottawa on the last plane before break-up. They have come to talk to us about bombs, they talk very loud and slow to us, like we are deaf and dumb, we smile at their silliness. I don't remember what the outside crises du jour was. Maybe they had excess funding that they had to burn off? We are told that in the event of a nuclear attack we are to put our hands behind our heads and crawl under our desks so we won't get hurt. "Try not to breath in the fall out dust as well," they say," it could be bad for you." "Okey, dokey!"

Today in the classroom a rumbling is heard, kids look slowly up from behind their books. Everyone is quiet trying not to breathe, listening intently. I can feel tremors in the floor; they must have sent those bombs. All eyes focus on our teacher, she hasn't noticed yet. "Teacher, teacher can you feel that?" little voices rise in excitement; she looks puzzled at the question and the unusual behaviour. We see a light begin behind her eyes…"Oh my god!" she exclaims (oh my god, this is a Catholic school and she swore, this is serious) the ice must be going out!"

Our ticket to freedom; books are dropped as kids rush to put on boots, to hell with jackets. Pencils are thrown back toward the mini bomb shelters, the big kids are running down the hall…"run, run the river is breaking up!" Bombs are forgotten, the break up of the MacKenzie is far more important than any southern politics.

The whole town is running toward the riverbank. A pole has been set up with a stop timer to record the actual time of break up; this will tell us who has won the ice pool. Where did all of these people come from? The total population of Fort Norman is less than 300 persons, they are all here. Anyone who can walk or be carried is sitting on the bank by the Hudson Bay Co., waiting to see if the river will continue to go out. Sometimes the ice jams and grinds to a halt. You may have to wait for days for this ripping birth of summer.

A warehouse sits a short ways from the store, it is filled with furs and hides that people have trapped and traded through the winter. Furs will go out on the barges and food will come in. Trapping is a lifestyle; it feeds kids and allows people to be responsible for themselves, a dignity that governments take away.

Giant chunks of ice 10 feet in depth start to push against stalled sister pieces of the same dimension, we have action. A winner of the ice pool is announced. From our perch on the banks high above the river we watch as the winters debris is carried north to the Bering Sea. The earth shudders as these colossal frozen blocks grind against each other, rise up and crash into fragments on the sheet ice below. The hill drops away to the north, several cabins are located on a bench below and to the right of us. Ice is now mashing its way up those lower banks, being pushed by the faster flowing walls that are straining to move down the centre of this massive river of silt and mud.

Our eyes are big as we look at each other with hands covering our ears, so much noise; there is thunder on the water. We smile as giant pieces of ice climb over each other and crash hard. When your world has no T.V. n o radio or boom boxes, a little bird's song is easy to hear, smashing ice is spectacular in volume.

Oh no, oh no…the huge ice blocks are crowding up on Granny Yakeleya's house. Closer and closer to her door they move, she is crying, "my house, my house!" All the people watch, their fear for Granny's home shows in their eyes, we can do nothing. Nothing can stop this wall of ice from grinding down everything that she owns, oh no! Slowly, slowly, the ice slows, inches to her door. "Please let it stop, please!" She starts to laugh, her wrinkled hands rising to cup her face. "I must have been good, see my house is still here, mashi, mashi (thank you, thank you)."

Everyone starts to laugh and smile, hands reach out to touch and pat Granny in her happiness, her home is safe. She will live by the river still. She has a willow stick that she chases us kids with. This river runs wild and hard. The murderous MacKenzie has expanded its maw and swallowed many people; Granny Yakeleya is determined to save us from ourselves. We listen to her because she cares about us, kids know these things. When we forget again, her willow will remind us. Mashi Granny I remember you still.

FORT NORMAN

SPIRIT OF SPRING

Do you remember when you were a little kid and an adult tells you that you have to do something that makes absolutely no sense to you? I mean even at an extremely young age you know better. But this is an adult and this is that era when grown ups were ALWAYS right. I remember thinking that possibly, when I am older, I will understand this, there will be a reason for this… I watch as my feet disappear under the mud, in the bath water, that is slowly covering my legs.

This mud comes directly from the tap; the blessing in this dirty situation is that it is warm mud. I know I would possibly pay for the benefits of this "spa" treatment now, but this makes no sense to an eight-year-old girl. Considering that we are miles downstream from communities who leave their garbage on the river ice over the winter, maybe not. Where does your spa mud come from?

It is shortly after the mighty, and in the springtime muddy, Mackenzie River has broken up. In the fall the men go down to the river when it has frozen into ice with a depth of two feet. They take saws and hand cut square 2 foot x 2-foot blocks of ice that are hauled to our icehouse. Inside the icehouse it is cool and damp even in the heat of the summer. Blocks of ice are covered with sawdust to insulate them and keep the ice frozen. This will be our drinking water over breakup.

My dad washes the sawdust off and puts the ice in a pail to thaw; a dipper hangs inside so you can take a drink. This sits in the kitchen beside our warm diesel cook stove. Muddy water from the Mackenzie is hauled to fill our water tank in the basement. These are the muddy waters that we "wash" ourselves, the dishes and our clothes in.

When the water settles it layers out into grey water and mud with grit. Sitting in the bathtub is an exfoliating experience. People from the north may have the softest butts in Canada. Am I clean? The towel certainly is not, do you sweat when you are eight years old? I don't remember, maybe it sloshed the sweat off of harder working people than me, I never felt

The Hunter, Joel Kostelnik

better for it I can tell you, and to a little girl it was disgusting bathing in mud.

My brother Joel has a gun, he is younger than I am, but he is a boy so he gets the gun. It's a 22 single shot rifle. The theory with rifles, knives, axes and every day items that could kill or maim, is to teach children to be the very best with them that they can. Rifles are not toys; the people or animals that you point and shot at don't bounce back up at the end of the game and start over… with a chance at more points. We know this; we have all been around when food has been shot with the gun. It is not a game, this is real and to shot something when it is not for food or use is not acceptable.

Little kids have to pack in wood for the woodstoves, they cut the kindling. They cannot drop the axe far enough to cut off a foot entirely. If you drop the axe on your foot or chop your hand when you are little and have any sort of brain cells, you won't do it again. At a very young age we know this. An adult who does this is another storey. It is the same with knives, how can you skin a rabbit or a squirrel without a knife? You tell me; it would be messy, lots of ripping and tearing, blood and guts. The fur would get wrecked. So learn how to do it right, you will live long and prosper.

Granny Yakeleya has chased us off the riverbank again. In the steep clay banks we have been digging up iron bubbles. These are heavy black balls that were spewn from bowels of the old volcano. They show up cannon ball size and weight. Odd shapes have formed, as the molten lava hit the water and cooled, we especially like to throw the round ones in the river. I wish I had kept one of the round ones; I have one that looks like rock poop. They are heavy so we get closer and closer to the rivers edge. "Zing" through the air swishes Granny's willow…yow, we scrabble for the top of the cliff, she will swat us if we are too close to the water, we deserve this. Feeling foolish we look for other entertainment. What about a picnic?

Kids scatter to find rifles and whatever we can "borrow" for our picnic. There are about twelve of us all under the age of ten that head off into the muskeg. Frozen cranberries attached to bushes on the ground and left from last fall are pounced on and devoured…they taste like medicine. We are heading for a small lake behind town to shot 'rats' for our picnic. An accumulation of gathered goods for our picnic reveals canned cocktail wieners, klik (mystery meat, we call it dog food) a commercial sized bag of cherry jello and the biggest prize of all; two cans of eagle brand sweetened condensed milk. Bannock is pulled out of pockets in pieces. It's a feast.

We build a huge fire and set out the tea pail for Labrador tea. Tannins from the muskeg have leached into the lake and coloured it to look like old tea already. It is better than the stuff that we have to bath in. Joel and Arnold have shot a muskrat each, that's enough. The boys skin them out and we skewer them on green willow and set them to sizzle over the fire.

Beautiful blue skies and warm, warm sun release the perfume of the bush. Willow is fragrant in the heat of spring, verdant morphs from colour to a scent that cannot be captured and bottled. It smells of baby willow shoots and musky moss collectively. Fermented berries add an acid undertone, drifts of Labrador Tea cause your nose to turn and follow this truly beautiful aroma.

Pick some Labrador tea and throw it in a pot of boiling water for tea or let it simmer to make your house smell like it should, a scent that connects you to the earth. Chemical scents are deadly and can never replicate Mother Earth's perfume. We drink gallons of Labrador tea as children, it warms you up.

My gumboot has a hole where a stick went through and stabbed my foot. Mucky water fills up this boot and when I walk through the muskeg it sucks my boot into the mud soup and pulls it off. I have destiny in mud. A tin can is washed out in the lake; pitch is cut off one of the conifers and the can containing the pitch gets set on the fire. This is gumboot repair 101, this method will seal birch bark canoes or patch most anything that needs it.

Once the pitch has melted, ash from the fire is stirred into the can with the melted pitch. No charcoal lumps can be used, only fine ash. It is almost too thick to stir and it is applied hot. A glob of it covers the hole and as it cools it is smoothed to conform to the boot. These are my only gumboots, there are no more to be found and no stores to buy new ones.

Bushes explode apart with people, in the quiet it sounds like a cattle stampede. Two- dozen young eyes look back at this out burst in total surprise. Adults are rushing towards us; the R.C.M.P. leads the charging cavalry. What's wrong? Everyone is looking at everyone else, the adults have stopped their charge and we can tell that their batteries have just run out.

"What are you guys doing out here?" We have a little cooked rat left and are hoping that they don't notice the eagle brand milk cans or the empty Jell-O package. I am sure that our brilliant red tongues and teeth would never give us away. There is no real food to offer, but there is tea… "would you like some tea?" one of the older kids asks.

"What are you kids doing?" the R.C.M.P. Corporal demands in his most military type voice. " Having a picnic, we are sorry there is no food left for you," is the reply. "Did you kids start a fire?" "Of course, we had to cook the rats!" "How did you kill the rats?" "With 22's for sure, only three shells pretty good ahey!" comes the proud response. The Constable turns and looks at our parents, teachers and friends, he has his back to us but we can see him spread his hands out like "now what?" He turns back to us and in the harsh voice he commands that we, "make sure the fire is out!" "Yes we will." "Very good," is his reply. "Carry on!"

Kids may not listen to what you tell them, but they will do EXACTLY what you do. And then what can you say? You had better teach them well. I don't know what the adults expected to find. We were doing everything that they taught us to do. They taught us well: to this day not one of us had ever shot the other and we still have all of our parts. My brother Joel was seven years old when he shot that rat for our picnic.

P.S. don't be silly, we weren't eating those long tailed vermin that live outside, we were eating muskrats, you should know that if you live here. Our rats are vegans and live in our crystal clear streams and lakes!

FORT NORMAN

THE VILLAGE OF WIDOWS

You complain that your life is too fast. That there is not enough time to do all of the things that you have to do, to see the people you have to see. If you truly want to slow your life down get rid of your cell phone, and your computer for that matter. There are few phones in 1966 in Fort Norman. Our phone number is three short rings two long rings; anyone can pick up the phone regardless of the ring, this is a community line. The telephone is wall mounted and built out of wood with actual metal bells, the handset weighs a ton. I can not say what it is made of, a heavy composite, it is not built for long conversations, your wrists would give out with the weight of the handset.

When you have something to say, you walk over and talk directly to that person. How can you pass information along without seeing each other's faces? Without eye contact and the shrug of your shoulders how can you exchange your true feelings? Your body language is lost without visual; someone could take your conversation totally out of context. It is difficult to hide body language. People can say whatever they want when there is no eye contact. Without standing beside the person you are talking to, we are removed from the situation and we become less responsible for what rolls off of our tongues.

As children there was nothing that we had to say that was important enough to enable us to use the telephone, we weren't allowed. Most of our friends did not have phones and if they did they also weren't allowed to use them. If I wanted to talk to Sarah or Eddie I walked over to see them. There were no fat kids, we walked or ran to get to anywhere. No one called or texts in the meantime to distract you, so you stay on course. From the top of the hill I can hear them "twittering" in the distance, sound travels well in this quiet time. The sounds of my friends playing on Fathers hill makes the sun shine brighter; their laughter is a different type of tweet.

Planes have been landing bringing the kids back from the hostels and schools elsewhere in the north, and slightly south of Fort Norman. They return from Grollier Hall in Inuvik, from Grandin College in Fort Smith and Akaitcho Hall in Yellowknife. Older brothers and sisters return after living away for 10 months. The only communication has been by mail. Everyone is shy, trying to reconnect. Little kids get sent out to the hostels if their families are too big and there is not enough food to go around.

The hostel kids come home with "fancy" clothes. They have T-shirts and jeans that look way different than ours; we have what ever the Hudson Bay Co., has on its shelves or what Mission people have sent up in boxes. Can you imagine, they wear their underwear (T-shirts) outside of their shirts for all the world to see? Some of them have words on the front, some have peace signs, ours t-shirts are Stanfield grey or Mackenzie muddy white, we keep this private article of clothing hidden under our shirts. They have bell-bottoms; the old ladies say it's a waste of material. "I could sew two pairs of pants out of that one wide leg!" "Such a waste, such a waste!"

My mother cuts pictures of clothes out of catalogues and sends the pictures to Woodward's Stores; Woodwards attempts to replicate the article in the picture. At this time Woodwards is the only store that ships parcels to the north. Sometimes they get close to what the picture is; regardless none of it was ever my choice, clothes were what you had to wear to keep the bugs off and the cold out. The latest fashion only served to distinguish me in a place that I already stood out in, I am looking for anonymity and my idea of fashion was distinctly different than my mothers.

"Do you kids know who the Beatles are?" "What about the Rolling Stones?" Painted black was the song of the day. 'What…you little bush kids, you know nothing!' 'We watch T.V., the Lone Ranger is a great show, you should see it.' 'We have radios and we drive around in cars, you kids are pretty dumb.' They talk different, we talk different, all try to fit the pieces of broken times back together in this little town of less than 300 people. Personalities jostle around trying to find ways to get comfortable in their skin and their homes again. Bumps and grinds, a fight breaks out. A smaller kid gets kicked out of the bed they have been using all winter… big brother is back, its hard to climb into bed with all of the other little kids again and Jimmy pees the bed.

"Tell us stories, tell us stories we beg." "Well, you have to be quiet and listen." "We promise, we will be good, we will listen." There are stores with every food that you can imagine, lots of chocolate bars and they have pop and something called pizza pie. Pizza we have seen in the some of the Archie comics that arrive with the big kids. I finally had pizza when I was in my teens. In the pictures, in the Archie comic books they showed them pulling it apart with strands of sticky white stuff still connecting it to the round "pie". I thought it would be sweet being called a pie, with stretchy strands of white taffy; the cheese and meat came as a shock.

They tell us grand tales of going to restaurants for chips and gravy, the stores have more than one style and size of gumboots…and running shoes. Sometimes they get oranges, their lives are amazing. They play basketball in a gymnasium and have school dances. Our mouths are as open in awe as are our eyes, they are so cool, they make us feel like the world is passing us by, we are missing all of this groovy stuff. They say groovy lots. Years later we find out that for some of them, life was not groovy at all in the hostels.

Yet they are starved for dry fish and dry meat and bannock. They teach us how to play baseball and we watch them pull cigarettes out of their sleeves and show us how they can blow smoke rings. "No, you guys are too little, but here take a pinch of this." A small can is rapped and opened with invitation. We should have noticed the hidden grins and sly eyes. "No, take a bigger pinch; put it in the front of your lip." Oh my god, it's terrible, we spit and cough and gag…teach you a lesson, never take snuff. I never would try that again! To impress them we would put a little dry coffee in our lip and spit. Yeah right you little devils! Good try, you don't fool us. You bush bunnies know nothing. We knew little of the outside world. Yet in truth we are all connected, the world is round, it is a circle there are no breaks.

This is a storey of that circle; this storey needs to be told again, in this day and at this time. Fort Franklin is located on the Bear Lake, across from a place that exists no more in structure, but lives on, a dark shadow in the water and the fish and the physical bodies of the survivors. Spirits roam human memories and live as well, "don't repeat the terror, don't repeat the terror," is whispered in the ears of those who will listen. One person can make a difference.

From 1942 until 1960 Somba Ke (the money place) Port Radium was a mining town.

Men from Norman and Franklin worked as coolies packing burlap sacks of uranium on their backs. The uranium was being shipped first by barge down the Bear and Mackenzie Rivers and then trucked to our Southern neighbours in the U.S. for the MANHATTAN PROJECT. It was one of U.S's secret operations with Canada and the people of the north unknowingly providing a basis for their plot. The Dene called the uranium "money rock".

Around 1990 it was disclosed to the people of the VILLAGE OF WIDOWS that the uranium had been used to construct two atomic bombs. The Village of Widows is also known as Fort Franklin, NWT, Canada, and now Deline. Fort Norman and Fort Franklin are villages woven together by bone and blood. One village is sister to the other with a combination of family members, family members that are dying from cancer.

Uranium has been dumped into the crystal clear waters of Bear Lake and travels its course through human bodies, native and white. White underground uranium miners suffered the consequences of cancer as well. Unknown to most northerners, these white miners returned south to their families and also died. An inquest into this wilderness of death was called.

A delegation of six elders travels from Fort Norman, to Hiroshima Japan. A celebration of peace is observed on the anniversary of the dropping of the atomic bombs. An estimated 220,000 people were killed when the U.S. dropped their atomic bombs on August 06, 1945 on first Hiroshima and then on August 09, 1945 on Nagasaki. Residual estimates of death and sickness cannot be tallied as it continues to this day. This is destruction that cannot be reversed; it cannot be "cleaned up". This destruction seeps into Mother Earth, poisons her heart and contaminates our very essence, the water. How can we live without water?

During the inquest into the plague of cancer in the Sahtu region the Dene learned that the uranium the men packed on their backs and some had died for, was in fact the uranium that went into the bombs that the U.S. constructed to destroy the people of Hiroshima and Nagasaki in Japan. THE MANHATTEN PROJECT.

Six Elders travel from a little village in the NWT, the first ore carriers (or their representative) of the uranium that went into the bombs meet with the first people of Japan on whom the atomic bombs were dropped. They have come to say that they are sorry. A Dene woman was heard to say," We are good people; we hope that blame won't be put on us because we had no knowledge about all that happened in the war."

Our friend Paul Baton a Chief and Elder of Fort Norman was one of the members of this delegation. He was a surviving ore carrier. My brothers Kurtis and John are his godsons. Once in a lifetime we are lucky to encounter persons of greatness, Paul Baton was greatness. I am honoured to have known him, Mashi.

P.S. Without choice the atomic bombs were dropped by the U.S. on Hiroshima and Nagasaki. By choice countries of the world now construct nuclear sites. Why do we commercially fish the mouths of spawning rivers? Why do we construct nuclear sites on earthquake faults? Why do we believe that we are god when documented history glares back to state that we are silly little beings when faced with the wrath of Mother Nature and her sister, Mother Earth?

We will not win by repeating mistakes. We cannot keep shitting in our nest; we do not have a replacement nest. All across this planet we are smart and compassionate people, we can do this, this is the only home we have, we have to do this.
NO WAR, NO NUKES, NO FRACKING!

FORT NORMAN

MISSIONARY: MRS. GRACE PRIEST

Summer is gone, fading quickly into fall and falling faster into winter. School has begun once again. Older students return to schools in the big "cities" of Inuvik, Yellowknife and Fort Smith NWT. There had been doubt that we would have a second teacher for the grades three, four and five kids. Without a second teacher, the kids in these junior grades would then have to attend school, probably in Inuvik. This means having to live in hostel accommodation for 10 months, there is no family contact other than postal mail during this time. Letters can be sent but many of the older people in the communities cannot read or write, they still sign their name with an X.

In the twelfth hour kids show up from bush camp, we now have enough students to qualify for a teacher and one is found. Parents receive the family allowance cheques from the government for kids that attend school. If you weren't a Treaty Indian it could be the only money you had to live on.

Older kids are happy to be returning to the bright lights of the big towns. Similar I suppose to trying to keep the kids on the farm once they've tasted the glamour of "city" life. Younger kids are more apprehensive about leaving home for the first time. It is an old tradition in Great Britain to send young children off to boarding school and for some not to return home for years at a time. "Residential" school or boarding school is still widely attended in the countries of the Common Wealth of Nations. Some things gained some things lost, choices have to be made, living in the bush is a hard way to go.

The town feels empty as the planes soar off into the skies. The propellers on the planes seem to suck up the last bit of wild and reckless that follows in the air behind the teenagers, it is too quiet on the dusty streets. We are lost, those of us left behind. We kick up rocks in the dust as we straggle home from the airport; we are weighted down in silence and loneliness.

TCK refers to children that have lived in two cultures and have assimilated both cultures. This term is generally used on children that are army "brats" or children of diplomats and missionary children that have lived in a totally different culture other than their passport country.

A period of only one year has been proven significant enough to cause assimilation depending on the age of the child. TCK stands for trans-cultural kid. A foot on either side of a cultural canyon that leaves your tender middle parts exposed to conservative ideals that disallow variance of any form. Causes tummy aches I assure you, there are many of us in the North.

On July 1st weekend we had left by canoe for Willow Lake to hunt rats (muskrats). At the junction of Bear River and Willow River we have to get out and portage the rapids. My kitty Sammy is with us, but not for long. He jumps out of the canoe and heads for the bush not to be seen again. We call and search the bush but he refuses to be found, Dad says we will stop and look for him on the way back; he will be much hungrier then.

I believe that the wolves will eat him. I cry all the way to Willow Lake. We did not find him; it is now fall time and is freezing at night. I think about Sammy and I wonder if he could walk over the sheet ice and come home before it gets so cold that he will be frozen.

The days are getting shorter, colder and darker as we settle into a quiet routine. One of the older girls that liked to pound on me has left for school, life is easier. Our new Principle is a musician so we get to focus on our recorders. A wild squeak and out of control treble are heard in the hallway, we battle to control these wild flutes. Mr. Mazur likes to sing to himself as he writes on the black board, he teaches us French songs.

Now and again we are let out of school early because the grey wolves slink into town. We all need to be at home before the dark falls; the wolves creep in with the shadow of night. When the wolf pack gets too brave somebody's Dad comes to school with a rifle and walks all of us home. The wolves come in to eat the dogs chained on the dog lines.

Loose dogs pack up and are worse than the wolves, we walk with big sticks. If we are lucky enough to find an old axe handle that is the best of all. An axe handle feels strong in your hand, it makes you tough. You're not afraid of the dog pack, you hold the old axe in your hand and walk backwards facing them as they try to sneak in and bite you. Show no fear, look big and tough and yell at them with a strong voice, don't trip, they will chew you up and kill you.

Mrs. Grace Priest is a Pentecostal missionary sent from the outside to teach us about Jesus. She is always called Mrs. Priest, her husband is Mr. Priest. Mrs. Priest talks funny, she is British. She wears a hat all of the time and wears dresses too. We see a pair of thick bloomers in one of the mission boxes; they look goofy but we hope they keep her warm. Sometimes her hats have jewellery in them and feathers, she is proper and teaches us manners. People send her boxes of clothes and material and wool to help her with her mission work.

A large box is filled to the brim with all colours of wool. Mrs. Priest has difficulty getting us to come to Sunday school; we are all Catholics after all. She decides that we should learn some lifestyle skills instead of church stuff. She is a very kind lady who has no children of her own, she loves Jesus very much, and she loves us as well.

We visit Mrs. Priest and she teaches us to knit, crotchet, sew buttons on clothes and patch holes in our pants. The large box of wool doesn't come with knitting needles, what to do? We are sent out to look for sticks that will replace the non-existent knitting needles. Green willow is the best of the worst and not very good at all. Mrs. Priest decides that large nails or spikes will work. She walks over and convinces Paul Baton that he should lend spikes to us. He agrees but maintains that he will need the spikes in the spring. They will be used to fix a house after we are done with them. We learn how to knit on spikes singing to the clicking rhythm of metal "Oh what a friend we have in Jesus."

Mrs. Grace Priest lived in the north as a Pentecostal Missionary for years. She was in her mid fifties in Fort Norman and carried on to do her work for many more years in the further north yet. She went to meet Jesus last June at the age of 102. In the Cochrane.

Alberta Newspaper there was a picture of her on her 102nd birthday. Mr. Priest had left on his journey first. I happened to be in Calgary when I received an email from my mother about Mrs. Priest and decided that I would go to visit her, it was then that I found out that she had already left on her next adventure.

This is Grace Priest running a scow up the Mackenzie River circa 1960's.

I always smile when I remember her patience with us little girls and our spikes of twisted wool. She smelled of mothballs and damp wool and somehow managed to have "tea" for us, which included homemade cookies. Her spirit was that of water, soft to the touch and unstoppable by force. She simply kept flowing around obstacles until she found another route on the way to her destination.

My Dad has found me another kitty, a baby with black stripes and sharp claws. We have had him for only a few weeks, he needs to learn to go outside to the bathroom, there is no such thing as kitty litter and the dirt is frozen. There is a surprise for me. Dad shows up with a bundle in a jacket. The bundle jumps with life, what could it be? Claws dig in and the bundle is dropped on the floor. A yowl escapes as it hits the floor with a solid thud.

Mad scrambling and with wild eyes out pops my cat Sammy! Sammy has no cat balance. The last barge of the season breaks up new ice on the Bear River. It is on its way to close down the NTCL camp up river. As the men watch the riverbank drift by they cannot believe their eyes. On the bank of the Bear River at the end of September is a wild Siamese cat hunched over the carcass of a dead duck. Sam refuses to leave the duck and growls at the bargemen in warning. They throw a blanket over him to trap him; they have to keep him rolled in the blanket to prevent being raked by his claws. He is a very thin cat and he is wild.

His first reaction in freedom is to try to kill the baby kitty with black stripes. Screams, Siamese cat howls and baby kitty mews for help, Sam's home! He doesn't want us to touch him; he walks like a panther, low slung with his mouth partially opened for scent, he is a feral cat. He creeps along the walls avoiding open spaces. We are told to leave him alone, give him time to accept us again.

In the middle of the night I sense a presence by my ear and a low rumble begins deep in a feline chest. He is on my bed beside my face. I hold my breath; I am not sure if he will bite me or lick me. He curls up and sleeps on my pillow. Tomorrow he will let me pet him I am sure. The poor little kitty needs to find another home. Sam will not tolerate him in the house and continually tries to kill him.

When company comes to visit we have to lock Sam in the bedroom. His favourite method of attack is launching himself off the top of the fridge and scaring the hell out of whomever he's landed on. His assault is made with full wildcat fury, complete with Siamese attack yowl.

Conformity is difficult when you have lived in freedom.

P.S. do you think that conformity may be the same as regulation…those were the days my friend, we thought they'd never end, but they are.

FORT NORMAN

PUPPY LOVE

Fasten your seatbelts, this storey jumps time and space and content, you are smart people you will figure it out.

Bored was a word that I don't recall using as a child or hearing other kids use either. My grandfather stated, "Idle persons had weak minds." "If you had nothing to do it was your own fault in this world of wonders. Right now we are wondering if stuffing candle ice and iodized salt into this old wooden ice cream maker will actually produce some form of ice cream. We all take turns hand cranking the handle. Our main ingredient is Pacific canned milk; we have sweetened the milk with white sugar.

Candle ice is rotten ice left over on the river banks after from the river has broken up; we have dug the silt covered particles out from under bushes on the banks of the McKenzie River. There isn't a lot of ice left, we should have thought of this two weeks ago when the banks were covered in massive remnants of ice from break up.

I am looking with trepidation at the old hand crank ice cream maker. There are about half a dozen of us kids at the Douglas house. They have a water tank in their basement because their dad works for the government. The water at the Douglass's has tasted bad for "awhile"; they now have an ice bucket for drinking water but are still washing dishes and clothes with the water from the basement tank.

My cat's name is Sam. He is a Siamese cat that I got for passing grade one. Sam promptly got distemper and nearly died. He survived, but was left with out some basic cat survival skills, he can't climb trees and when you hold him tummy up and drop him he doesn't flip and land on his feet like a cool cat should, he hits the ground with the thud of dead weight, directly on his back. He can hold off three sled dogs though, as long as he had his back in a corner. Poor Sam has been the only cat in town for months now; the Douglass's have a Siamese cat also but haven't seen him for "awhile". I am hoping to bring Sam over for a visit. There is a great possibility that if a dog hasn't killed that other cat a roaming wolf pack has.

I recently read an article in one of the Whitehorse, Yukon Territory newspapers, an editorial letter about people negligently letting their dogs run free from their chains with the suggestion that this enabled wolves to kill them. I have to say that the NWT wolves preferred to come into town and kill the dogs that were chained up, this may have been easier than having to chase the dogs down I suppose. (Probably a different breed of wolf over there)

Back to the old hand crank ice cream maker that I am trying not to think too much about. It has been determined this afternoon that my cat Sam will be the only kitty in Fort Norman. The Douglass's cat has finally been found, in the silt at the bottom of their water tank. To our fascination, there is only a funny little skeleton left, Mrs. Douglass threw up. I am hoping that they haven't washed the ice cream maker in months. We produce a grainy slightly runny canned milk ice cream that is MARVELOUS!

We are at the bottom of the barrel today in all regards. Firstly finding the disintegrated kitty and now resorting to a game that we play at the Douglass's when there is absolutely nothing left to be thought of. Remember, we have no T.V., no movies, no video games and no radio. We get tired of board games that no matter what they are called most often end up as war. We have a new game. I am having difficulty trying to describe it so that it can be printed and read by the general public and then I realize that there are way more important things in this world that need to be dealt with other than the protocol in this storey.

I hadn't had much experience with little dogs. It wasn't until I was in my twenties that they started to show up in my world. My first encounter with a fou fou as I call the little darlings was at a dinner party in Whitehorse. Dogs in my time were meant for work, the concept of feeding an animal that didn't work is amazing, what do they do? What are they for? They are very cute, rather noisy and seem mostly agitated unless held and petted and fed continual little "treats."

These "fou fou's" are unsettling to me and I attempt to reach out and acquaint myself with this critter. It responds by licking my hand and wanting more ear scratching, I have a new friend. I am not paying a lot of attention to the fou fou now, absently rubbing his ears and engaging in conversation with the people at the party. There is silence in the room, as I re-focus, I begin to realize that my leg has acquired a moving attachment; I try to quietly disengage the miniature Romeo without drawing too much attention to the situation.

With classic mating attitude, the more I try to disengage, the more he "loves" me. To hell with being polite, suppressed laughter is exploding from behind hands and I climb on top of the chair. Genghis Khan is strutting below me growling with unrelenting lust. "Oh my little boy you are so precious, you are such a loving little dog, but I suppose we will have to stop embarrassing our guest…no shit, what exactly is the protocol for avoiding dog lust at a social function?

Sheba, the Douglass's blue-eyed Siberian female is a very "loving" dog as well. The difference is that she outweighs Romeo the fou fou, by at least 80 lbs. She is chained just off to the side of the front door, testament to the fact that other than her over zealous libido she is a kid friendly dog in a kid infested house. Our challenge is to run through her chain line and not have her "catch" us. To have Sheba as an attachment to your leg meant she was attached to the rest of your body as well, she out weighed most of us. If you did get ambushed, somebody had to help to get her off, the ultimate insult, and it felt like hours of humiliation before you could escape the love of Sheba.

The big kids (eight and nine year olds) are constantly trying to escape the drudgery of babysitting younger siblings, today is not that day. Today we have been stuck with one of the four year olds. You know the kind, if we don't do what he wants he'll tell on us, if we don't give him most of our ice cream, he'll tell on us, this little miscreant holds us hostage.

Sometimes revenge is so very sweet. Does anyone want to play that game with Sheba? "I do, I do!" he yells. "But you can't its game only for the big kids." "I'll tell my mom on you," he challenges. Wel-l-l… OK, but you had better be sure, it can be dangerous, it's w-a-y-y too dangerous for a little kid." "You have to let me!" he demands…FINE…we explain that he just has to run through Sheba's chain line and get to the other side without her catching him, it is pretty easy after all.

Sheba is jumping at the end of her chain and grabbing air in excitement, I don't know if she sensed a victim or just fed off of the energy that this game is generating. "Are you ready?" " Set?" " Let him go!" He doesn't make it two feet and she's on top of him in a frenzy of dog love. Now what, he's bawling like the world is ending. God maybe she's bit him or something, he shouldn't be crying that hard. Quick get him out of there if one of the adults hears him we're going to get the willow. Man can that kid can scream! Two of us decide that together we can distract Sheba and get this kid out of there. We are afraid that he is hurt for real, he won't stop his screaming.

Once he is safe and away from Sheba we search his arms and face for bites, we look for blood, my god his mother will kill us, he's her favourite. For crying out loud shut up and tell us what is wrong with you! He hic-ups and coughs and finally bawls out these words, "I DON'T WANT TO HAVE PUPPIES!" we HOWL!

P.S. Hello to everyone at the Gold Pan Saloon, in Whitehorse, Yukon. This was a special request from Tom B.

FORT NORMAN

THE GIFT

****THIS STOREY IS RATED PG NR (PERSONAL GUIDANCE, NORTHERN REALITY) THIS IS ABOUT KILLING FOR FOOD****

Winter is a long drawn out affair in the Arctic. The men stick gamble and play cards, they laugh at each other and drink thick, black, sweet tea well into the deep dark of the night. Everyone hopes that old man winter leaves before the firewood runs out. Dogs are used to haul wood and there is no chain saw. Firewood is cut with an axe and Swede saw; this takes time and uses muscles. The snow is sticky and makes for hard hauling for the dogs.

Water is carried in buckets from holes chopped in the ice. When the ice gets too thick, chunks of frozen water are chopped and melted by the stove in buckets. Everything is people powered. Women and kids set snares for rabbits and traps are set for rats (muskrats). We cross the river that is about a half a mile wide in front of Ft. Norman. In freeze up and break up we balance long poles across the front of us. If we fall through the ice we hope this will keep us from dropping through the frigid caverns and into the raging Mackenzie River below.

Of course, the best trapping grounds are always on the other side of the river. Bullets cost money, it takes a skilled hand to reach in and grab a live rat that is hurt and not get bit. The rat is held by the scruff of the neck and the tail; with a sudden jerk the backbone is broken. Killing snared rabbits is a bit more gruesome and personal. You have to reach up under the rib cage of the warm bunny and squeeze its heart until it stops beating. Food really does arrive live, this is reality, if you choose to eat meat something has to die.

In the springtime we are all ready for fresh meat and something green for the Moola's (white men). Living food is a dream from the south. There is no salad; there is no fresh fruit and no fresh dairy, what does a real egg taste like? Barges bring in your food order in the summer. Shopping is

done once a year, you have to be organized. If you forget the flour this is your fault and there will be no bread for your family for the year. When you need bread, you have to bake bread.

Fresh food that arrives on the barge only lasts a short while. Eggs can be dipped in vegetable oil and or turned every few days to make them last for up to six months. I will tell you that by the time they get close to the four month mark they smell too bad to eat, I don't care what anybody says. We use powered eggs, they are terrible and they don't taste like egg.

A genius somewhere spelled milk backwards to read Klim; this is supposed to be a great marketing scheme. Klim comes in big tins, when you scoop it out it squeaks like chalk; it is always lumpy on the porridge. Pacific canned milk diluted half and half is a luxury, we get to use that for the first few months after the barge comes in, when it is gone we go back to Klim.

Canned potatoes canned cocktail wieners, just think about it… canned bacon is marvellous, so is canned butter. Canned grapefruit is something that I would buy today if I could find it. Crosswell and Black canned cakes arrived with friends from outside. People who have lived in the north would bring produce in with them if they came to visit. You could tell who had spent time in isolation; they came with fresh tomatoes, oranges, bananas and milk. These are dry communities and if a few cases of beer or a bottle of whiskey came in I was too young to know about it. There were always brew pots perking under someone's bed. A yeasty smell of fermentation sometimes overrode the wood smoke and eau due unwashed body as doors opened wide to let spring in for a visit.

Huge cans of peanut butter separate into peanut oil and peanut brick. You have to constantly flip the cans to try to mix the two. Dried potatoes and onions are excellent after they have been soaked and fried. Meat is fried in inches of lard, people crave fat. Dry meat is drug through the butter can. Store bought meats like pork have a high fat content and go rancid quickly even though they are frozen. Foods such as this have to be eaten first, by spring time there is no variety and anything left at the bottom of the freezer will gag you and we eat it still, there is nothing left. Fresh meat would be a gift.

A hum passes through the town. Moccasin telegraph is real. People gather together on the riverbank, an expectant silence… "What is going on Alvin?" I ask my friend, "be quiet Moola ya," he whispers," your voice carries across the water of the river and grows to a shout on the other side." The Mackenzie River has opened up from the winter freeze. Break up of the river has just happened.

Anticipation is a vibration through the crowd, I am excited and I don't know why. A sharp crack is heard from across the river and then another one catches the echo of the first. Rifle fire, a gun is being fired. At what, at what, I can hardly stand it. I can't talk and everybody knows what they are shooting at except me. Ahhh, the crowd lets out their breathe in unison, they got it, they got it. "Got what?" "Please Alvin tell me!"

"They shot a moose on the sand bar right across from town." His voice is proud. This is such a gift; tonight we will feast on the riverbank in the dusk of a not quite midnight sun.

Firewood is being gathered and piled on the riverbank. "Don't cheap out!" someone yells, "make a real fire!" Four foot logs are stacked on top of the starter fire and a tri-pod it set up with chains to hang the ribs up to get touched with smoke and black. Coals glow and light up the body of the moose that is laying close to the waters edge now. It is not yet Solstice so we are in the grey of twilight. You should see how quickly the moose hide is coming off.

A murmur passes through the people once again. This is a cow moose, a pregnant cow moose. Her unborn calf was near term. A second gift, elders with no teeth are looking towards the heavens with thanks. Everyone is hungry, and nothing that is left in town can take away that feeling. Bum guts (lower intestinal tract) with its nutrient rich lining is needed to take this hunger away. The calf hide will be tanned and bleached and used for baby and ceremonial clothing, First communion slippers for the Moola ya maybe, the calf hide will be bleached white in the sun.

A single drumbeats and low chanting spreads through the crowd. The big fire blackened ribs are cut off the chain tied to the tri-pod and passed around. Smiling faces catch the glow of firelight. Brown hands reach out for their share. There is no lemon soup here, people wipe their hands on the rocks, and kids rub the blood off on our pants of course.

Dogs are howling in chorus, they each have their own song. A lead dog starts and dogs with their own pitch, add depth to this wild harmony. Dogs howl at feeding time, they smell the meat cooking and want a share. Drums set them up as back ground vocals and the combination of beat, chant and howl is raw and real, goose bumps run up my arms and make me shiver.

There is a small bit of soapy fat on this cow, people are cutting it off and eating it with their eyes closed in ecstasy. Raw liver is passed to the men who shot and hauled this gift home. Eating together beside the river connects us all; this feast of fresh meat drugs people almost to sleep. We lay in the glow of fire on the banks of the Mackenzie River with wild dogs serenading us; no one wants to leave for home.

Brains are kept to cure the hide. A huge tongue flops around in one of the boy's hands as he chases the older girls with it making them squeal. He gets a smack on the head from his mother, the tongue is a delicacy. Nothing is left on the beach. Leg bones will be roasted and cracked for the marrow; the Chief gets the heart and head. We have all chewed on pieces of the rubbery nose. The moose needs to be cut up and divided among the people.

Stray dogs are trying to steal leftovers, this is dangerous, they could go into a fighting frenzy and someone will get chewed up. Sticks are picked up in defense; an axe is waved to keep these wild things at bay.

Slowly we start to leave. Everyone carries chunks of raw meat. Little kids stumble up the banks with their bloody burden. You need to learn young how to take care of yourself, you have only you to count on. If you need food you have to kill it, if you are cold you have to haul wood and build a fire. When you are self reliant, you are ALIVE and you are STRONG. People are proud, maybe I do belong here a little bit, this little white Girl.

P.S. for my first communion I did wear a pair of beautifully beaded slippers made from soft white moose hide, trimmed in white rabbit fur. Soon after I passed these slippers to another little girl. She wore them on her pathway over the northern lights were she went to meet her ancestors, I remember you still Gloria, dream well sweet baby girl.

FORT GOOD HOPE, N.W.T.

SO YOU THINK YOU ARE "NORTH"

My first conscious perception of North and South came years ago at Marsh Lake. I was visiting my friend Verna at the time. Her father Charlie Taylor asked me when I had moved "North" to Whitehorse. I remember considering that perception, I had not prior to this question. I replied." this is actually a move south for me." It was not the answer that he was used to.

This concept drew boundaries in my mind that had not existed before. I knew that I lived in the north, but to me the north was anything above the border of the Territories, not a consideration within those boundaries, and anything above that imaginary line was home.

The White Girl Series starts in Fort Norman on the Mackenzie River, NWT, Canada, in 1965. In 1789 Alexander Mackenzie canoed the then "River of Disappointment," to the Bering Sea. His disappointment being documented in the title he assigned to the river. Sir Alex had hoped that he would reach the Pacific Ocean via this route.

Fort Good Hope is located on the Mackenzie River a northern stones throw to the Arctic Circle, roughly 100 kilometres north. Whitehorse, Yukon is about 900 kilometres below the Arctic Circle and Dawson City is 445 kilometres south of that chilly line drawn on paper maps. Just so you know, Whitehorse in comparison to the rest of the Arctic is pretty much south! There is a whole other world of North above us and east to the rising sun.

My first visit to Whitehorse was in 1972 for the Arctic Winter Games. A DC3 loaded with participants flew south from Inuvik. How excited we were laying in the ribs of that plane flying to the big southern city of Whitehorse! I won a gold ulu at those Winter Games. That White Girl dancing with the Mackenzie Delta Drum dancers, well it was me. It took days of scrubbing to get the brown shoe polish off of my face. I was the source of much laughter I am NOW happy to say.

The White Girl Series will continue from Fort Good Hope almost on the Arctic Circle to Kugluktuk (Coppermine), well above the Arctic Circle and finish in Inuvik, 200 kilometres above that frozen imaginary line. I am trying to give you a perspective here.

A friend of mine Don Mackenzie of Sechelt, B.C. is a tugboat Captain who has travelled the world's oceans on ships and monstrous tugboats. His father Captained barges on the Mackenzie River when Don was a boy, in the 1940 era I believe. Don has a fascination with the Mackenzie River. We talked about my life on the river and about the book that would and should come of that experience.

I had been kicking horse turds for months when he cornered me one day and said, exactly how is that book coming along?" "Well," I said, "I think I am going to approach Jim Butler at the Whitehorse Star and see about doing another column for him." (I was finishing up the Adventures of the Audrey Eleanor) It will be called the White Girl Series; I wanted to test the waters.

Depending on how you grade "White", I most certainly was the fairest skinned girl on the Mackenzie River in Fort Good Hope, Fort Franklin and Fort Norman over the age of four. White families generally left for the South when their kids came of school age, we were the exception.

Don Mackenzie's reply was, "it's pretty hard to write about people when they are still alive isn't it?" He had poked his finger right into the centre of my eye! That's exactly what I was dragging my feet about and not realizing it. It's real easy to write about people who are dead; they do not in my world at least, phone you up or email you and say, "That was bullshit." To date that has not happened. As we all know when we look back and have the glory day discussion, everyone has his or her own version of your memory. Once again, these are my memories, not to be confused with anyone else's, level on the level.

These are true stories. This statement is directed specifically to Dan the drywaller from the Okanogan. It had not occurred to me that anyone would think otherwise. Dan commented on the White Girl Series one-day stating that I had a great imagination and the stories sounded almost real, but could not possibly be true.

Northerners will recognize the little nuances and klim milk dustings over the verbiage. I was not considering the New North where these realities no longer exist, this influx of outsiders.

To you in the Subaru, with black synthetic clothes covered in white dog hair, the red kayak a hump, the bike spinning, spinning on your rump… those were the days my friend, we thought they'd never end, but they have. We walked, ran and paddled to get to where we had to go, not to recover from a long day behind the desk, but to get there, to make time, to live. You come behind us and create your own frontier with its differences.

Those of us who lived this life and in this era were lucky, it will not come again. We cannot be duplicated. You will talk of your day in time, for now you get to read of mine. (I'm a rhyming fool today)

Fort Good Hope has a current population of 463 residents according to Wikipedia. My guesstimation in 1967 is 350 people. It was established as trading post in 1804 by the Northwest Company. A young priest from France, named Father Emile Petitot was instrumental in the design and décor of the Our Lady of Good Hope church from 1864 until 1878. The church was professionally restored and declared a National Historic Site in 1977.

As a little girl with my mind numbing through the drone of Latin mass, little fingers gently traced brush strokes swept on hand hewn boards by ancient hands: of old colours dyed with berry juices, fish oils and ash. My head thrown back marvelling at the stars covering the ceiling, a smack from an elder brings a swift return to the weighted gravity of latin reality.

This is a difficult place for me to write about. Fort Good Hope was a hard road to go. I want to remember the light and bright of places, my memories here are hard stroked by death and harshness. In a small village death is personal, you know everyone and everyone knows you. I hope that as we go along what I write will trigger brighter memories.

Good Hope was known as a village lost in time; it was like going back 30 years in the then 1960's. With no road access and only long river travel in the summer, travel was restricted to flying either to the "Wells" with connections to Yellowknife or Inuvik and points south from Yellowknife. Connections with the outside world were extremely limited. No one flew to the towns unless you were sick or had to go to school. Fly to Yellowknife for a visit or to shop, such an idea!

There is an ancient path from Fort Good Hope NWT to Mayo, Yukon. People walked from one village to the other in years past. As the Raven flies it is 450 kilometres, walking over land and across rivers I suspect you can almost double the distance. If you could manage 7 kilometres a day under packs, it would take about 62 days one way. It could probably be walked one way in the summer and the return done the following year.

We are lying in the moss picking cranberries with the older women. They talk to us about the bushman and men in general.

"No, no don't take all of the berries, leave some berries for next year." "You girls think you're tough, you know nothing, nothing." "Haul water, chop wood everyday is nothing, you cry babies." "In the old days, in our mother's days, they pack everything, everything!" "Them women get worn right out, nothin left of em, and they were young and strong and nothing left, nothing, nothing." "Life was so-o-o-o hard, you girls go to school, learn the new ways, don't be some man's pack dog." "In old days woman was a pack dog, be better in your life." "They walk all-l-l the way over the mountains to that other place, then they come back again, so hard that old life, so hard."

The bushman, well that is another storey.

P.S. even to this day, after living in the Yukon for 37 years, when someone asks me where I am from I go to auto default and say Fort Good Hope, NWT.

FORT GOOD HOPE

BACK IN TIME 1967

Word comes down from the gods that are the new NWT Government, the Kostelnik family has to move to Fort Good Hope, NWT. This will take us three hundred and eighty miles north to the Arctic Circle and closer to the Arctic Ocean. My father's title of Indian Agent will be no more when he starts work in Fort Good Hope. With the new government the title of Indian Agent changes to Area Administer. John Kostelnik is the last Indian Agent on the Mackenzie River and possibly the last Indian Agent in Canada.

People in Fort Norman exclaim that the people in Good Hope are backward; they live like it was a hundred years ago. This is an observance from a community that still uses dogs for transportation and has no outside communications except by VHS radio at the RCMP or the Church. The conversion to skidoos has begun in Fort Norman, but definitely not in Good Hope, we are slowly leaving the Stone Age and climbing into the age of technology in 1967.

My father becomes mobile with the arrival of his "boys" from Wood Buffalo National Park. This retired team of dogs are his only reliable transportation, the bombardier always breaks down and there are no gas stations, this limits travel. You can only travel as far as the gas you can carry with a motorized vehicle.

Dad has spent much time running his dogs on a circuit to Willow Lake and across to Fort Franklin. His last return trip to Norman is taking longer than expected; my mother asks a bush pilot flying back to the Wells (Norman Wells) if he could make a detour over towards Franklin to try to spot my dad. His radio call confirms that my dad is still a day out and that he must have trouble with a dog because he has a loose one running at his heels.

It is common to let a dog run loose if he has hurt himself. This is no dog; a huge black timber wolf has been looping behind my father for two days. He edges the camp at night and follows close behind during the day. Dad says the wolf is not aggressive, but he feels like a lab specimen with the wolf acting as a scientific observer. The wolf wants to know more about this clumsy being that requires four dogs to carry him down the trail.

They are travelling companions, this lanky wolf and the solitary man in the lonesome wilderness.

Once the river is cleared of ice and debris my dad will load the boys, his dogs in the canoe and move them to Good Hope. My mother, brothers, Sam the Siamese cat and I will fly over in the DC 3. We have to wait for the ground to dry up enough to allow the plane to land on the dirt airstrip. Packing means taking our few personal possessions. It is too expensive to move furniture and household belongings so the government houses are fully furnished right down to the cutlery. People who have lived in government housing know the red maple furniture that filled these houses.

Pieces of this furniture pop up at garage sales, battered but intact after years of many families usage. I bought an old government, red maple kitchen table and chairs from my friend Reba Miller who is moving to Australia. I hope that she and Gavin and Mauve have a smooth adjustment from Marsh Lake in the Yukon to Darwin, in Australia. I will take care of the table Gavin; it feels like home to me too.

The last movie of this year, which has been playing for the entire month, is Joan of Arc. The last movie before break up gets re-played until a plane can come in and finally take it away. In the summer we don't watch movies, everyone is too busy to sit still that long. Nature is much more interesting and being stuck inside is something that you have to do if you are sick. Why would you stay inside if you weren't sick?

I believe that my mother has been strongly influenced by the Joan of Arc movie; she clips my hair as short as the boys. My name is Dawn, which doesn't sound different than "Don" except in my mind and now I have a boy's haircut. All of the girls wear their hair long and straight. My friend Sarah has beautiful wild curls, a throw back from a French voyageur ancestor I am sure, her last name is Gaudet.

The teasing is limitless. Maybe the haircut will provide a cover for me while we try to adjust to a community that is not real fond of White people. Girls can be much crueller than the boys sometimes and I make a cute little boy with my short hair. They may leave me alone until my hair grows out and they discover that I am actually a girl, and then the "fun" will begin.

It is treaty day in Good Hope. People collect on the grass in the RCMP compound. Treaty Indians receive $5.00 per person and sometimes a wool blanket. Non-treaty Indians receive nothing, which isn't much less. Everyone is dressed in their finest, woman's heads are covered in bright scarves; they wear long dresses and sparkling beaded mukluks with rubbers. Some of the old men sport old black top hats and black suit jackets that look to be a hundred years old. Hundred-year-old hats perch on heads that look to be a hundred years old also.

Women chew snuff and spit as well or better than the men. Kids roll around on the grass between the people that are sitting cross-legged waiting for the Government Officials to finish their buzz. Slavey sings its song in the background. The drone of voices puts everyone in a trance. Look… look …down by the church. This is 1967, Canada's Centennial Year.

IT IS OUR ONE HUNDRETH BIRTHDAY! Expo '67 is being celebrated in Montreal.

Down south of the church is where the river barges land. Look, look what is that coming? Tinny music carries over the water and begins to drown out the government propaganda. A huge yellow wheel with bright accents wobbles as the barge bumps into the dock, the music becomes clearer.

What is it? Come… come quick, all kids are running at full tilt towards this spectacle. The barge people are turning up the music…such a thing, such a thing! What is it? We are not allowed on the dock. The elders walk ever so slowly down the hill. Top hats are distinctive against the blue of the sky; we have to wait for them, to show respect, we wait. They are so-o-o slow. We can hardly wait, we mustn't talk either. Slowly, slowly they approach the water.

"What is this thing White man?" one asks. "Why it's a Ferris wheel, haven't you ever seen a Ferris wheel?" the barge guys ask? What does it do? "Well, you get on it and it goes around and around in a circle." "For what?" "Its fun, it is to give you a ride high in the sky and back again, you could touch the stars if there were any in this land of midnight sun."

The bargemen open the gate to the swinging chair and demonstrate how to get in and sit down. Black Top Hats say nothing; we are squirming, if they don't like it we won't be able to try the ride until someone can convince them that this is OK. That decision could take longer than the barge will be here.

A sweet smell trickles back to the dusty hot land, "hey you kids try this stuff." One of the men balls up a pink fluffy thing and throws it towards the kid pack, a scuffle occurs and a dirty pink orb is held triumphantly aloft by an older kid. "Eat it." "Really?" "Eat it, its sweet." The kid sticks his face full into it and bites, he smiles back with pink teeth, the kid pack tears what's left of the dirty pink ball apart, what is this incredible taste?

Haven't you kids had cotton candy before? "No." This is the Centennial Barge travelling north to the Arctic Sea, stopping at every village along the way. The elders with the Top Hats are getting into the chairs on the Ferris wheel, the chairs creak and sway in the wind, the old men in black hats attempt to maintain their dignity and balance….and this storey will continue in the fall.

I know, I know but its so much fun to leave you hanging. Part 2 of this storey is called "Touching the Outside".

P.S. Adios Amiga's/Amigos we are called back by the siren song of the Audrey Eleanor. (See the Adventures of the Audrey Eleanor also on this website) She waits for us in the Sun on the Sunshine Coast.

Powell River and Texada Island boast the most temperate climate in Canada, with less rain than Victoria. In Pendrell Sound the seawater reaches the same temperature as the West Coast of Mexico. This is in Canada my friends, no passport required, no borders to cross, this is our home. This is our playground. We cannot let Audrey go, so we need to find a different path.

We will drop our anchor in front of Rosebank Cottage by the Sea, a wonderful B&B owned by Karen and Clarence, you can goggle this site. We will sit and drink lemonade on the deck of Rosebank that over looks Van Anda Bay and decide what we want to be when we grow up. (You know that I am lying, we will be drinking beer, we are going to miss the Yukon Brewery growlers) Texada Island is such a beautiful place; they have no bears there, after living on an old bear trail this spring I look forward to their absence.

I have had encounters with eight bears this spring. One of them would not leave my doorstep to allow me to get to my car. When I yelled at him he simply cocked his head and sat down outside the door. What do you do when the bear won't go? I went upstairs and had a nap. When I woke up the bugger was having a nap also, just over in the green grass by the septic field. Not enough distance away from my doorstep to allow me to make a run for the car.

I yell again, this time I am pissed off, he must sense this. With a dirty look over his shoulder he ambles away with a look that translates into, "what's the big deal, I only wanted to visit!"

These stories were all published in the Whitehorse Star Newspaper. The storey that concludes this one is called "Touching the Outside." I have opted to keep this series close to the original publication.

FORT GOOD HOPE

TOUCHING THE OUTSIDE

(PART 2, THE CONCLUSION TO BACK IN TIME)

Around and around they go, around and around. When will they stop we want to know? A river barge decked out with a Ferris wheel is docked along the banks of the mighty Mackenzie River beside the village of Fort Good Hope in the North West Territory of Canada. It is 1967 Canada's Centennial year; our incredible country is celebrating its 100th birthday, such a young strong nation are we. As part of the celebration a barge with a highly visible Ferris wheel, a cotton candy machine and the live "rock" band the Centennaires brings "civilization" and a touch of the outside world to these isolated communities along the Mackenzie River.

Around they go, around again. The Ferris wheel slowly moves the old men in black hats out and over the swirling back eddies of this mighty river. Black top hats are worn in honour of treaty day, which has coincided with the Centennial Barge. The old brown eyes beneath the top hats see our frustration and keep going and going with eyes crinkled at the corners, laughing in their fun. On the outside they are stern old men with tall black hats, looking straight ahead. They sit high and proud in the seats that swing and sway in the wind and the wake from boats passing in close to get a better look.

In our young minds they have been taking up our space in those seats for days. We are being taught a lesson, we must learn patience and we must learn respect. Not one kid dares to say out loud any of the words that are threatening to dance off of the tips of our tongues. Just let us have one turn is pleaded out of many, many dark brown eyes in the crowd. There are a few pleading blue eyes as in the crowd as well, but very few.

Cotton candy is tossed out for all kids to try. It is magic this soft pink cloud of sweet that melts away in your mouth. The food barge is late in getting to town; there has been no candy for months now. We make sugar candy in the winter and throw it in the snow to harden, but lately have resorted to buying the small jars of Heinz baby food for a sweet fix. The baby food costs too much to feed a baby with, which is why it is still on the selves at the HBC.

It is expensive; we all stick our fingers in the tiny jars licking and reinserting fingers yet again, there are no "double dipping" rules at this party, I don't recall being sick very often either. We share all that we have. Eagle brand condensed milk is a distant dream; next to raisins it is the first to sell out at the Hudson Bay Company. Our teeth and smiles are pink; hands are licked clean of sticky pink mixed with dirt. Sweet pink smells (it does so) of cotton candy mesh with the salt and buttery aroma of popcorn, they have popcorn too!

What a celebration, a grand birthday party, wow look at all of the treats, there is pop in bottles as well, little coca cola bottles, they are so cute. How can we go back to normal once this all leaves? This is a very special birthday party for our country of Canada, for all of us who are Canadian.

Finally, the elders decide that they have tormented us enough; we have been good kids watching them go round and round with faces covered in sticky sugar and popcorn salt. Not one word is said in disrespect, the reward of the ride is sweeter than the cotton candy. Anticipation has already built this ride into legend, in the actual short time that we have waited. This storey of the Ferris wheel will be recounted throughout the winter, the seats will swing wide and wildly out over the Mackenzie in death defiance as the storey is told and retold. For now we all sit very quietly, big eyes meeting wider eyes in excitement. Our knuckles are white on the metal handle that keeps us from falling out. We hold on for our lives!

It bumps as it starts and we begin with a swinging jerk, it stops, it creaks, it groans. Oh no, it can't be broken, our hearts will be broken! The man pulls and pushes levers and with a hard jerk and metal grinding on metal we slowly reach out over the edge of the barge, now there is only water below us. A whimper is heard from a really little kid, a hand quickly covers the small mouth, "Sh-h-h, its OK, its ok, we are having a ride to the stars." This is whispered loudly to the little brother.

Most everyone in town has no experience with motorized equipment and there are only trees to climb that will not ever get us to this height. There are very few skidoos, no cars, Roy Corliss has a truck I believe and my dad "borrowed" heavy equipment off the barges every chance he thought he could get away with it. Travel was done on foot or by dog team.

Our lives are in the hands of the deckhands and this creaky old machine that is taking us way out, up and over the swirling back eddies of the Mackenzie River. The "wheel" is stopped when the first passengers reach the top. We can look way-y-y down to the ramparts. Movement makes the seats swing, we are all too nervous to cause that on purpose, yet.

Cautiously we strain to look back over our shoulders to catch glimpses of our tiny village; it looks a little different from up here. Shoulders start to drop as we relax," I can see my house," is repeated back and forth. Voices begin to rise in confidence, "ahma, ahma look at us (mother, mother) we are so high up here, its fun!" "You should bring granny and come for a ride!" " Deh, deh, come, come and try, you can see the whole world." And it was the whole world.

The Centennial barge was launched in Hay River in the NWT. It was a combination of two 115-foot house barges. On board were exhibits from the1967 Expo Pavilion in Montreal. Consideration was given as to what would be of interest to the secluded people on the "River." A vote was taken and the decision by the local people is that they most wanted to see a live milk cow. It was determined that to take a cow on the trip from Hay River to Tuktoyuktuk on the Arctic Ocean created a huge challenge, no one grew cow food along the banks of the Mackenzie for one thing.

The trip is 1,800 kilometres long and will take the whole summer to complete. A Ferris wheel became the second choice and as a 9-year-old

The White Girl in the foreground with Stanley Cook, Tony Granjambe, grooving on the banks of Jackfish Creek, Angelina Rabesca facing the camera in the background.

kid who waited in line time and again for a swing around the world it was a much better selection. I can't say that I remember much of the exhibits.

At night the Centennaires come ashore and play live and recent music for us to dance to. I love to dance and was asked to do a demonstration. I am nine years old; my experience is limited as I attempt to remember dances that I had seen on television years ago…when I was six years old. My grandparents were beautiful dancers and had taught me how to do all of the old fashioned waltzes; I knew that this is not what they were after. There is no radio or television, some of the kids that go to the hostels in the big towns can do some groovy moves but none of the town people had seen anything except drum dancing and jigging.

Seconds after I am persuaded to get up on the dance, every other kid in town is up on the dance floor as well, strutting their stuff, the music is incredible! This dance becomes an icebreaker for me. We have just moved from Fort Norman to Fort Good Hope, everyone is staying very distant.

Prior to us leaving Fort Norman my mother had cut my hair very short. By the time the Centennial barge arrived it was growing out. My name is Dawn, which sounds like Don to people other than me. I was mortified when one of the elders smacked me upside the head and said in disgust "hey, you better get a hair cut yere startin to look like a girl."

My theory had been that if everyone thought I was a boy life would be simpler; in fact they all thought that I was a very strange little boy. While this had saved me the occasional beating, it had also ostracized me and the summer this far had been pretty lonely.

Angelina Rabesca, Janet Manual and Helen Codzi took pity on me after the Centenaires dance and let me tag along. My elementary knowledge of Slavey enabled me to understand some of what was being said. When it was discovered that I could "talk" a little, life became easier. It also enabled me to get out of 'Dodge' if need be.

Being a moola sha or molla tu we (Whiteman's kid) did not automatically win you friends and salutations; I learned to run like the wind. Later I became pretty good with my fists. English was only spoken at school and a mix of Slavey slang and English was spoken in our house between my brothers and I. It is 1967 in a small village on the Mackenzie River and I am the only White Girl in my school. I climb the hill toward home often with frozen tears and a bloody nose.

FORT GOOD HOPE

SCHOOL DAYS AT THE DUMP

I remember when I walked five miles through snowdrifts that were up to my butt; packing my little brother on my back cause he didn't have any shoes. All we had to eat were potato samwitches made out of crumbling home made bread, scooping snow to melt in mouths when we were thirsty, you kids today don't know how easy you have it.

Isn't that how that old whine goes? Well, in Fort Good Hope we had to walk a mile to school. There were two choices of approach. One was to climb the staircase that leads us up past the Corliss's house, the alternative shorter and much more dangerous route is the short cut through the town dump.

We are little kids; we walk to school in total black in the winter, there are no streetlights. The rule is that school commences up until the temperature drops to -40f. It is an amazing trip to school at -35. You have to run so that you don't freeze your mukluked feet, (feet in store bought boots of that era would freeze in fifteen minutes) but you cannot breathe in the cold air so quickly that you freeze your lungs.

I tuck my face sideways in the hood of my parkie and breathe in the warmer air that my breath generates. My left ear has been frozen time and again by leaving it exposed this way, it's better than freezing your lungs. We run mostly because we are scared. Starving sled dogs pack up and attack. A dump in a poor community contains plenty of nothing, the hole in the doughnut as my grandfather used to say. What tiny bits it does have, attract desperate wolves, skinny, snarling dogs and all manner of critters that scavenge.

Huge ravens open shiny beaks to curse us as we pass, they are impossible to see in the dark and we clump together grabbing at each other in fear. Their raspy harsh calls screech inside our heads, sound carries sharp and crisp in the cold.

Helen Codzi lives the furthest away from school. Her father is the special constable for the RCMP and they live at the RCMP compound. She walks to my house then we walk to our friend Angelina's. Safety is in numbers and we walk with an old axe handle for back up. My brothers Joel and now John walk with us as well. John Jr. is finally old enough to go to school.

In Fort Norman he would stand outside of the classroom window hoping someone would let him in. He was pitiful to see with his nose red and running, begging to come inside, we can't look at him, we feel so bad. Sometimes teacher lets him in, she might as well let him in none of us could work knowing he was out there freezing anyway.

The boys wait outside while we go in to get Angel. During the night the fire has gone out in her house, there is no smoke coming from her chimney. You need to step down to get in through the door. Some of the older houses are sunk into the ground to help insulate them from the cold. It is so very cold in her house; and dark, it is colder inside than outside. "Angelina," we whisper trying not to wake up Janie, her little sister.

How come they haven't frozen in the night I wonder? Every morning I am afraid that I will find her frozen. She sleeps with her two little sisters and her mom so they keep warm. Her mom tells her and Cecilia to go ahead, she will light the stove. The water is frozen, there are no lights, the kerosene lamp will be lite when we leave, we are late. There is no time for her to eat.

I believe that my friend is so strong; she goes to school every day. Every day she has to chop wood and heat up water to wash and to cook her food, she has an outhouse that is never heated and it feels like -40, when it is only -20. She is very proud, so I don't tell her how strong I think she is to live like this. I have a warm house and running water, everyday I know I'm lucky.

Angelina and I are best friends, we are also each others competition in school…who has the best penmanship, the best spelling, she has much better penmanship than I do and does to this day. She laughs uncontrollably when I try to sing. She tries to warn me if I'm going to get beat up again. It's not easy being friends with a mouthy little white girl I'm sure, she teaches me words in Slavey.

Smoke hangs low over the village. A candle or kerosene lamp gives up little glimmers of light along the black road to the school. Other kids are late this morning; the air is so cold it hurts to breath it. Frozen leather bottoms on our "shoes" allow us to half run and half slide as we go. The group builds as we head towards the school, everyone has their noses tucked inside so they don't freeze, there is little conversation.

It is still pitch black, we look at each other as we hit the juncture to the dump, should we or shouldn't we? We are late, let's do it. Quickly, quietly, listen, listen…faster, faster, we are running on our tiptoes, we want to get through the dump before something hears us. Wait, what is that sound? We all know this sound, were is it coming from? "Over there," someone whispers, we try not to speak. We close in on the sound and our fears are confirmed.

The whimpers are almost under our feet. We all know what has happened here, we all know what is supposed to happen, what do we do? Destiny plays itself out as our decision hangs in the balance. We are still children after all, how can we not do what we do. An older girl bends over and picks up the box of hours old puppies. Lets take them to teacher; he can take care of them we decide. Tiny baby dogs mew and grunt, they are almost frozen; they must have been left to freeze just before we got there.

Teacher, teacher look what we found in the dump this morning! Our teacher was new to the north. He has great difficulty with isolation and the over all concept of survival. He does not believe that there is no television or radio, he spends several days when he first arrives trying to set up antennae's that will capture even a ghost signal from an outside world that will make him feel less isolated. He becomes depressed when he realizes that he cannot make this connection.

"Barbarians," he screams, "I can not live with these barbarians anymore!" He grabs the puppies from Martha; he doesn't know what to do with them. They are whimpering loudly now as they warm up. We don't know what to do either, we didn't mean to be bad and the teacher is still yelling something about heartless animals, we decide we should go home. We haven't even warmed up yet.

There are no veterinarians on the Mackenzie river. Dogs did not get "fixed" because there was no one to fix them. When a female dog comes in heat she is brought into the house or put in a pen if you were lucky enough to have a pen. Stuff happens and puppies happen, so what do you do with the puppies?

Personally I would prefer freezing to drowning. Bullets cost money and were needed to shoot food. Some winters people are hungry and dogs starved, dogs that did not work did not get fed. So what to do? Letting the puppies go to sleep in the cold was probably the most humane choice given the options that were available.

We go back to school the next day and our teacher is there. We feel sorry for this man who does not belong. He looks at us as if we are an alien species; we were to him as he was to us. It is a long year in this classroom.

From that day in February on, we do not go through the dump again. The longer route up past the Corliss's house poses fewer problems. Long steps with platforms have been built for us to climb up the hill to the school. The Corliss house is midway up the hill on a level plateau. Mr. Corliss is a contractor who lives there with his wife and two small daughters, who are too young for school.

You can imagine our surprise when one bright spring morning we climb the first part of the hill to find that a D-6 Caterpillar is parked on the hill side with it's blade stuck in the front wall of the Corliss house. My father never claimed that he could operate heavy equipment very well.

FORT GOOD HOPE

FISH CAMP IN THE RAMPARTS

Frank Pierrot

Just south of Fort Good Hope NWT, the mighty Mackenzie River squeezes itself down into a comparative trickle between towering limestone cliffs. The Ramparts becomes a bottleneck during the spring break up when 6-foot vertical chunks of dirty block ice grind into the limestone banks. Narrow canyon walls channel the mass of thundering ice; they clog and crawl on top of each other.

Pushing and shoving the angry packing ice reaches heights of 20 feet or more. With a sigh the narrow opening slowly closes and the water level in the river north of the white limestone begins to drop. There is a gigantic frozen plug damming the river. We hear the screeching and grinding of the massive cubes of river ice as it fights to escape to the sea. Debris from the winter is churned in the mix; garbage from the southern communities blends with splinters of northern spruce "pecker" poles.

Shudders in the earth signal a break in the pressure. Groaning, screaming blocks of frozen Mackenzie River slam each other in their race to be first out of the jammed chute. Massive muddy blocks push smaller pieces under and into the river bed as they grind and fight their way north to the Arctic Ocean. In awe we watch this spectacle each spring as the Ramparts spews out this mass of frozen muck. Sitting on the riverbank high above the river we feel secure. With the river ice finally gone, travel between villages and to summer fish camps begins.

Andre LeCoue former Chief of Fort Good Hope on the front right

Pauline and Andre La Coue have their fish camp on the north end of the ramparts. Andre was the chief of Fort Good Hope when we first arrived to live in this tiny northern community. I love to watch him string his nets in the early spring sunshine before breakup. With fish line wrapped around a homemade wooden spindle he weaves it back and forth through the nets repairing tears from the previous years fishing.

Andre's hands dance through the squares in the nets, he never seems to follow their action. With eyes staring off far, far into memories, his fingers fly back and forth. He and his wife Pauline have lost all of their children to tuberculosis I believe, I don't know how many, and I never wanted to ask, any child lost is so very significant, more than two is not imaginable, how can you survive such tragedy. Their faces are imprinted with a sorrow that had carved deep grooves into their soft brown skin.

They walk with a quiet, slow dignity that makes me feel like I am watching people who have been climbing mountains for years. Pauline would hold my face in her worn old woman hands; they felt like soft worn tissue paper. She would look deep into my eyes. She never said anything to me when she did this, she would smile and pat my face. I wondered if she was looking for a daughter in my eyes. Souls don't differentiate between brown eyes and blue eyes.

It takes time for the river to clear of mud and junk before the nets can be set. We are finally going to La Coue's fish camp! I love visiting Pauline. Their fish camp is well set up above the river in between the limestone. I swear I can smell the fish as soon as we are in the canoe. My brothers are a pain; everyone jostles for a seat, my mom yells at us to sit down for "god's sake!"

There are no lifejackets and the Mackenzie is still at full boil. I scramble for my favorite spot in the bow of the boat. My dad pull starts the kicker and it roars to life. Sunshine warms the spray of water as it splashes our faces. It is not far to the ramparts and we look at each other in trepidation as we approach the towering limestone. This is where the bushman lives!

Pauline and Andre are the only ones that I know who live on the doorstep of the bushman. No one else wants to go into the canyon. "Listen, listen for a whistle, just a lon-n-g low single whistle." "You girls hear that, run like hell!" This is the call of the bushman. The bushman needs a woman to take care of him, to scape his hides, make him clothes, cook for him and have his children so his lineage can continue. (Other archaic cultures attempt this practice as well) If the bushman catches you and you escape from him you will die in two years. If the bushman catches you and keeps you, you will probably die from overwork or childbirth in a much shorter time.

A bushman is huge and black and covered all over with hair. He creeps around the edge of camp watching for silly girls that do not listen, or grabs women who go too far out to get firewood by themselves. Legend ranges with thoughts that attached him to the White People's stories of Yeti or Sasquatch, or to the possibility that these were black men who escaped from the south and now lived at the edge of the light of campfires.

There was talk of Black Men from the south that came to hide away from their worlds. Black men who are sick of the wars that never end in the land of the "free" and home of the "brave". Living in the frozen north, stealing a woman and becoming a "bushman" must seem an easier battle than being shipped off to fight a political war in Korea and Vietnam that kills innocent woman and children and leaves them to live with the remnants of their souls forever tortured by a fight that they did not believe in.

All that I know is that while playing out in the bush, I would get that hair rising on the back of my neck sensation, goose bumps would raise any skin that was hairless and a dread feeling that I needed to run somewhere fast became over whelming. A sense of fear would permeate the crowd of kids. Like a flock of ptarmigan we panic, scatter and run for our lives to the town, arriving breathless and feeling silly. Looking at each other in the security of the village no one wants to talk about their fears.

Lets go over to Helen's to warm up and have tea. Slowly, slowly we get braver. The toughest kid says, "That must have been the bushman coming in for kids." "We escaped him again!" I never saw the dark form that some did, I can only state that this feeling of panic did happen, it arrived with an instinct to run for survival that was primal and real. This basic instinct keeps me alive to this day. When you feel it, trust it, scatter like ptarmigan.

Nets are set in back eddies to catch whitefish; sometimes a coveted Loch snakes its way through the weave of the net and gets entangled. I think a Loch may be like a catfish or fresh water Ling Cod? It has a tail like a snake that wraps itself around your arm when you are pulling it out of the net. A giant whitefish called a Coney would show up on occasion as well. We want to catch whitefish to make dry fish. It is so good; Pauline makes the very best in the world.

She cuts the whitefish so that the skeletal section remains in one long piece that is still attached to the body at the tail end. The flesh of the fish is laid out in one flat piece and scored with a knife into cross sections so it will dry nice and crispy. The belly has the best oil. Pauline is patient with a little girl who is all thumbs. It's hard to separate the bones from the meat and still have it looking like it once was a fish. I struggle to make my fish look like hers, it will take years and I don't know if I could get even close to my 10 year old expertise anymore.

With the bone attached we hang the fish on poles that are set up on racks. The bone anchors the body to the poles and stops it from falling to the ground. A small fire is built under the fish to keep the flies away; it gives it a light smoked flavor as well. About 120 of these fish are piled and stacked, then bound tightly into "bales" of dried fish. These bales were used for dog and people food. In the ancient times fish bales were used for trade with other tribes and the HBC. This type of dried fish is almost impossible to find anymore, it has a totally different taste from smoked salmon. It peels beautifully from the skin and tastes like nothing else, you can also put it in water and make soup, I prefer it peeled right off the skin, wonderful.

Once in desperation I tried to duplicate this dried fish by substituting ocean going white fish for the Mackenzie River whitefish and using cedar cause there was no alder willow for smoking. I was pregnant at the time and not on the Mackenzie River, if only I could have simply craved pickles and ice cream. It just DID NOT work; there is no substitute for Pauline's dry fish. I also made dried meat out of southern deer and it did not come close to dried moose, it was a rough nine months until my son arrived.

P.S. Chere the Bear Wilson in Dawson City wrote to tell me that she likes the White Girl Series. She walks across the now frozen Yukon River to get to town. She stops by Max's to pick up her copies of the Whitehorse Star that they save for her so she can read my stuff. Thank you Chere, I needed that.

FORT GOOD HOPE

OH DONNA

Alexi is dead! What do you mean Alexi is dead? He was here this morning, I just saw him he can't be dead. No, those guys were out in the river and he fell overboard. That river took him, he's dead, he's gone. It can't be. Alexi works with my dad, he is a terrible tease. He sings stanzas of "Oh Donna, " to me. It's true; they just put Alexi's body in the town freezer. Alexi did not count thirty years on this earth.

An oppressive weight settles over the village, drums pound, low chanting fills in the quiet spots. The throb of the drums is the heartbeat of the earth. It feels like Mother earth is expressing her sorrow with the low heavy beating of her heart. No one is in the streets. We are told to stay in the house until my dad can figure out what is going on. He is gone for a very long time, I am now afraid that something has happened to my dad.

Today you kids will stay inside. My dad has come home. We never stay inside, what's going on? Alexi's family will remain in their house while three of Alexi's friends haul water and chop wood for them for three days. Drums remain a constant pounding in the background. The friends check the snares and traps and bring food to Alexi's family.

People start to move around on the second day after Alexi's death. Everyone is sad, we all knew him well. Father Guitar, a nickname us kids call him, is running around the village screaming that we are all heathens and savages. In the winter he zooms around town on his yellow broomstick shaped like a skidoo. His long black "dress " flapping out behind him. The engine on his skidoo is on the back; he gets his "dress" caught quite often in the belts. He imperiously tells us in heavily French accented English to "get me out!" He is best left alone.

Last winter, Father Guitar hauled me out of my chair in the rectory at the end of a slide presentation on a Catholic Mission in Mexico. The jest of the presentation was to get the very poor people of Fort Good Hope to donate money to the very poor people of Mexico. We saw pictures of grand cathedrals with statues gilded in gold, chalices of pure gold and golden candlestick holders.

Father Guitar asked if there were any questions after the slide show. In my ten-year-old mind I could not rationalize this whole procedure. "Why doesn't the church sell some of their gold to feed those poor people?" I ask. "You stupid, stupid girl'" he screams, swooping down on me like a skinny black crow, his cassock flapping out behind him. "Out with you, out with you!" I duck, but he manages to grab my ear. Muttering in French he drags me down the aisle and throws me out of the front door of the rectory. An earthquake sized crack splits asunder my faith in organized religion at that very moment. I no longer want to become a Nun. At the age of ten this rational made no sense to me, in this age of "wisdom" it still does not.

My very best friend Angelina and I are stopped on the road in the village by Alexi's three friends, she does not want to stop I can tell. " You girls come." I don't know what is going on. These are friends of Alexi's and they have tassels of braided wool in beautiful colors. Angel is very serious and very cautious; she looks carefully at the tassels and picks an end. Slowly, slowly she pulls the wool. "Ah-h-h!" I can feel her relief; her piece of wool is very long. "You must do it now," I am told; I still don't know what the purpose of this is. Blue is my favorite color this week, I choose a blue end and begin to pull slowly, the tassel releases a length of blue wool as long as Angelina's.

Mahsi, mahsi we say. "What did we do?" I ask, Angelina says," the length of wool we pull out tells us how long we will live." "We will live a lo-on-ong time," she smiles, "we will be old women together my sister!"

We are such good friends; we decided last winter that we would become true sisters. I have only brothers and Angelina's sisters are very little. How do we become sisters? You have to cut yourself and mix your blood of course, everyone knows that. It is a very serious commitment. Both of us decide how the vows should go, we get a sharp knife and cut our palms.

This is not a pinprick; we cut our palms at the base of our thumbs. Blood drips into the snow, hers and mine. She is brown, I am white, our blood is red, same difference. Red drops against white snow, we clasp our hands tightly as the blood continues to drip…we are sisters for life.

To this day she has changed very little, my Sahtu Sister, not even much

Traditional Sahtu area beading on a white hide purse

grey! Her husband is Joe Grandjambe, I knew him first as "Lolly" a name from childhood that will stay forever in my mind. Mischief lights up his eyes, especially at the mention of "hockey". They have many children and grandchildren. Angelina's grandchildren call her Nan. This is what my grandmother was called. Angel has carried this tradition over with her children as a tribute to my grandmother. She and my grandmother were soul mates.

When a little Hareskin girl from Fort Good Hope was longing for her home from a far away place, Nan made Angel her favorite comfort food. My grandmother's special version of macaroni and cheese. We were visiting my grandparents in Lethbridge, Alberta; it is lifetimes away from the mighty Mackenzie River. And the tiny village of Fort Good Hope.

Drums are beating in my head; the whole world is filled with the throbbing of the drums, my god will they ever stop! They will be taking Alexi to the graveyard soon. Father Guitar has said that he won't allow the burial in "consecrated church ground" because of the pagan rituals that have been practiced. We are heathens and savages, no one is attending mass He is not popular to begin with; the anger in the village is thick as wood smoke.

Terse words amongst the adults are said quietly so the kids don't hear. We can feel the cut of the sharp edges as the vowels drop to the ground and shatter into shards that we walk on with caution. They penetrate us regardless. People are mad. The drums continue, people whisper that Alexi's unborn child is walking through the town in the early morning, crying and searching for his father.

We now have radio. Music from the outside world is playing in the tiny village of Fort Good Hope. The request show is heard from Yellowknife, we crowd around listening to our friends and family sending each other songs through the air. Did you hear that? Terry sent a request to

Charlie; she's in love with him again. Holy, what kind of song was that? "Little arrows in your clothing, little arrows in your hair," some guy named Leapy Lee is singing this song, we laugh, we know their business now; everyone knows their business now. Nothing will be private anymore with the request show! Our world has changed forever.

I am not allowed to go to the gravesite. My father says that he doesn't know what will happen if Father Guitar refuses to allow Alexi to be buried, it could be dangerous. I stand at the kitchen sink washing the dishes. In front of me outside of the kitchen window, just a few feet away are the doors to the community freezer were they first put Alexi. They have taken him away now. It doesn't seem real that he will never tease me again. The radio is playing beside me on the counter. " I had a girl and Donna was her name, since she's left me I've never been the same," croons across the airwaves. I hang my head and cry, Alexi is gone.

FORT GOOD HOPE

THE SPIRITS OF RELATIONS

Raw winds rip and tear at a tattered hide that barely keeps the old lady and tiny baby from being frozen. The remnants of a fire sputter and threaten to extinguish itself with every blast of frozen winds. Old moose and caribou hides have been thrown over wind fallen trees. This shanty provides temporary protection from a storm that has caught a small family out on a snowy trail in winter. They are heading back to spring camp after a long and arduous wintering in what used to be good hunting grounds at Colville Lake. In this year the caribou didn't come. An old moose succumbed to the bitter winter and has provided tough and stringy meat in the dark days of winter solstice.

They have dried the remaining meat from the old moose to take on their journey back to the spring ratting grounds. This method of preservation helps to eliminate weight and preserves the food indefinitely. There are five in this family group, the hunter, his wife and five year old daughter, his mother and a two-month-old baby. This boy child has been long in coming. An older son had died on this trail three years prior.

The Hunter's mother is old for her time having reached the antiquity of 48 winters. Her bones hurt; she has walked hundreds of miles and carried many heavy packs in her long lifetime. Now she struggles to keep up and she slows her family down. Spring is late arriving and this last battle with the frozen gods of darkness and cold may claim them all as they run out of dried meat.

The little girl is collecting firewood while her mother checks the rabbit snares. Nothing, nothing it is too cold for even the rabbits to stir. The hunter makes a wide circle around their little camp hoping to stir up game. A fat squirrel is something to be dreamt about, but they are still sleeping and would be skinny anyway. Skinny squirrel would be a welcome meal right now. There is not enough food to feed the five of them, it is still a week's travel with good weather to rat camp, the food will be gone in three days.

Whimpers from the baby make it difficult for everyone to sleep. His mother's milk is dwindling; she is unable to produce enough for him on the small amount of food that she has to eat. The fire is stoked, feet are kept as close to the flame as possible, bodies are compressed together to conserve heat. It is difficult to leave the warmth and glow of the fire without disturbing the rest of the family.

As hard as it is, the old lady has to leave the shelter each night to relieve her bladder; it is part of the nightly routine. Tonight is different; tonight she will leave on a much longer journey than the brush at the side of the lean to. She hums an old travel song under her breath. Goodbyes were said to her grandson as she sat alone by the fire cradling him. Her heart sends messages to her granddaughter, daughter –in-law and son. Saying goodbyes face to face would cause her family more grief then she can bear.

Her journey to the stars is hers to do alone. With one less mouth to feed there will be more for the rest, allowing her grandchildren to survive and carry her spirit with them. Her soul soars with the thought of her gift. She senses a change in the weather. Blue moonlight on black trees casts long black shadows on the snow. Humming her travel song she walks into the face of the moon.

Trudging and stumbling through snow that reaches almost to her hips she begins to tire. She has to be far enough from camp so they don't find her. They know her gift and will only look long enough to be able to console themselves with the fact that they have looked. She is their mother, so they will try, they will weep and they will live because of her gift.

So tired so tired, frozen feet begin to warm. The snow looks soft and inviting, all the hurts are leaving as heat spreads through her worn out body. Her song breaks loose and she allows it to slip off of her tongue and carry gently through the trees and drift up to the moon. Careful, careful sound carries for miles at -40, she does want company, she has come many miles to sit in the light of the moon.

Ah-h-h its time to sit and rest. She is so very tired; it feels wonderful to be warm after months of frigid black winter. Here the blue light of the moon is so bright that she believes this must be what is warming her. Her face illuminates in the moonlight as she sinks into the deep snow, her back supported by the old spruce tree. "My friend, let my old bones rest against you as my spirit fly's to the stars." Her request is to the tree, "I do not feel alone with you holding me."

Sleep makes her eyes heavy; her last memory is of the flashing of blue and green lights that dazzle and dance below the stars. They have come for her; the northern lights have come to carry her to the stars. She will return home to her ancestors. "My children live and carry my spirit within you always." "Be happy and dance in the light, I am not hungry and my feet are warm."

Later that spring a mother bear breaks though the last bit of snow covering her den. Winter has been long; she has birthed two cubs this season and is starved from feeding them without having any thing to replenish herself. She is desperate for food. Late spring means that the young green things are only thinking about showing their parts to the world. Bugs and other crawly critters are not about to move through the snow this early. Not far away from her den she spots a ragged bundle propped up under an old spruce tree…and yet again, the mother's gift gives life.

"You kids!" "Hey smarten up running 'round the muskeg like that, make noise, bang on the trees with sticks, let them bears know yer' here." "Watch for that bushman you girls." So we are supposed to be noisy for bears and quiet if we think a bushman is here. Adult controversy is a mystery to those of us under the age of twelve, talk about mixed messages. What were we most afraid of? I was more afraid of the bushman than the bears. Although bears would hunt us if they were hungry, they were only bears after all.

People smelled bad to bears according to the old people. By spring I have to say things were ripe in our village. There are few washing machines and almost no indoor plumbing. They had to be pretty hungry to want to have one of us for a snack. (We are little kids) But stuff happens and we need to let them know where we are so they can avoid the smell of us and we can avoid running head on into a "brother."

Bears are our brothers. To kill a bear is not a decision made in haste. Bears are not hunted for food. Why would you kill something just to kill it? How sick is that? You only kill for food and you give thanks for that gift. Bears had to be killed if they were being socially unacceptable. If Bears are violent, cause destruction of property or steal food, they are killed. Food raids on tree top caches by bears, cause people to starve in the dead of winter.

There are no detention halls for bad bears, or holding cells. No psychological analysis or observation, as in the case of Trevor the dog. Social services and Mae Bachur animal shelter haven't had legislation passed in order to rehabilitate them, yet. If you are a threat to the rest of your world you need to behave or accept real consequences, even bears are held responsible for their actions.

"Ah-h-h our brothers the bears, they are clowns." "They fall in the river, they fall down the bank in the mud and they are surprised by themselves when they are silly." "We do not eat the meat of our brothers." "Sometimes our brothers ate our ancestors. In the old days people died on the trail, the ground was too frozen to dig up dirt to cover bodies.

"See our little trees?" "Pretty hard to put a person up there." "Ancestors of animals that eat meat may have eaten our ancestors, we do not eat those animals." ' A part of our ancestors remain in the spirit of the bear, the spirit of the wolf and so on.' "This is why we do not eat them.' "This is the respect that we give them.'

P.S. I would like to tell my daughter that she has the spirit, strength and wisdom of a bear, a Kermode Bear, I am very proud of you. (She is currently in Whitehorse, I am onboard the Audrey Eleanor)

FORT GOOD HOPE

WE'LL BE HOME FOR CHRISTMAS

We are going to see Nan and Gamp for Christmas! We are flying outside, I can hardly believe it! I have not seen my grandparents for three years. These are my paternal grandparents they live in Lethbridge Alberta, Canada; we live in Fort Good Hope N.W.T., also in Canada. It is 1,500 miles to travel to Lethbridge for the holidays.

Our trip will take us from Good Hope by Otter (plane) to Yellowknife, N.W.T; we will overnight in Yellowknife and then fly by DC6 to Edmonton. In Edmonton we rent a car and drive to Lethbridge. Travel this far, at this time of year takes a very long time. Today it is quicker and easier to get to Australia.

We have fancy parkas for the trip. My mom has asked Lucy Jackson to do the embroidery on our new parkas. Lucy also helped my mom sew the stroud pieces together. Stroud resembles felt, it is very expensive and hard to get. These are beautiful "parkies" we also have new shoes. Mukluks are called shoes; we are pretty groovy in the far north. My shoes aren't new, but they are a fancy beaded pair that my mom got from Fort Chip, I have been bugging her for years for them. They finally fit me.

We even have new duffels; these line our mukluks and are made from a thick wool material. My brothers parkas are in navy blue stroud, mine is done in red. Our baby brother Kurtis has fox trim on his parka. Fox fur is best for small kids and for dress parkas for ladies, it tears easy, as does rabbit fur.

Around the hoods on the men's parkies the trim is usually wolverine with the feet and claws left on. This frames out the men's faces and it doesn't freeze and frost up as bad as wolf does. Wolverine is a masculine fur, women mainly use wolf or beaver, Beaver doesn't frost up easily either. Rabbit fur is nice and is used mostly for baby clothes or to trim out slippers that aren't used outside. Rabbit is a very delicate fur; the hide is thin and tears easily.

In Fort Good Hope the people were known as the Hareskin Indians. They snared rabbits in their area and made beautiful blankets and clothing out of the rabbit hides. They would rough tan rabbit hides and cut them into strips. Scrapping a rabbit skin with a knife is akin to scrapping tissue paper with a knife. These strips would be woven together with the fur side out and each little square would be hand sewn. I only ever saw a little baby blanket done like this and it was very old. The patience and skill to work with rabbit hide this way is legendary.

My dad's jacket is unbelievable. I can't remember who made it, but it came from Fort Franklin. It was done in navy stroud with white stroud as a background outline. The back yoke and two front panels were embroidered in magnificent multi-coloured flowers that covered his shoulders and chest. Fringes of cut stroud crossed his back, his chest and down his arms.

The quality of the embroidery work on shoes and parkas is judged by the women of that day by how many strands of silk are used to embroider, as well as the choice of colour combinations and design. Work done with two or three strands of silk was considered superior and the women who did this were outstanding craftswomen within their own communities.

My father's jacket was a masterpiece. Unfortunately this jacket disappeared when we moved to Whitehorse. My father took the jacket in for dry-cleaning and our family never saw it again. I hope that whom ever "borrowed" it realizes its value. By the way, we would like it back if you are done with it.

Yellowknife is so very cold with the wind howling off of Great Slave Lake. We stay at the Gold Range Hotel known by northerners as the "Strange Range. "the only hotel in town; I don't think I have to say more. There is KENTUCKY FRIED CHICKEN in Yellowknife, can you believe that? We each have a glass of milk to go with the chicken, it is almost real milk! Freight costs were actual in those days, we are drinking tri-milk which is a concentrate (less weight) that you add water to. It's the best we've had in years!

In Edmonton the temperature is 14 F, (about -10 C) we have had a cold December in Fort Good Hope with temperatures running at -27F(about

-33C) for the first part of December. 14 F is spring weather to us. Our cousins in Edmonton watch us in distain. We are having a snowball fight on their front lawn; we have stripped down to our T-shirts. In the 1960' s T-shirts are considered to be underwear. With no heavy layers to weigh us down we roll in the snow like fools and laugh…its 4:00pm in the afternoon and it's still light! We are energized.

Our cousins are wishing that we were way less visible, "there are neighbours and have you heard how these squares talk?" It's downright embarrassing; my dad calls it our northern accent. It has taken me four years of university English to round out my northern accent and in a minute of talking to someone from the "River" or Old Crow it sings its way back into my throat and my tongue lets the slur of it slide out of my mouth in an easy soft and beautiful song.

We have a rental car. Kurtis and John Jr. are quiet: this is not usual. "You guys, you guys look!" In total awe they slowly wind the window in the car up and down and up and down again. "Look, when we turn this handle the window goes up and down, h-o-l-y!" They are four and six years old and can not remember being in a car. The car goes scary fast, then we get used to it and yell at my dad to do a roller coaster.

He comes up fast to a hump in the road and coasts over it, leaving our stomachs at the top of the little hill. Four kids fight for two windows. Kurtis stays up front with our parents and Joel and I get the window seats. Oh groady, I only have the window open for a second when a spray of aromatic slur covers my face. Dad is spitting snoose (snuff) out of the window, it makes a brown streak down the side of the car and across the window, we don't dare open that window. We now fight over one window.

My grandparents are surprised; they aren't expecting to see us. I am so very happy to see them; I miss them terribly when I am so far away. We exchange letters as regular as the mail allows, sometimes the letters get lost and there is no contact for months. They live in a tiny house with three small bedrooms and one bathroom upstairs. Their kitchen table can seat four only with a lot of effort. There are six of us in my immediate family. My Aunt Delores, her husband Budge and their three kids are coming for Christmas as well.

Thirteen members of our family will take turns with one bathtub and one toilet, there is no shower. Seven kids sleep on the floor under the

Christmas tree, I have no idea how Santa managed to get those presents under the tree without being caught, but he did. Santa is magic after all. Not one of kids has emotional issues because we had to share one toilet and sleep with our cousins under the Christmas Tree, honest. I can't say I would have remembered if there had been an extra toilet or a shower. These are some of my best childhood memories.

A long table is set up between the living room and dining room for Christmas dinner. To get anywhere we have to climb over the chairs. We are Slovaks, our celebration is days of food and family, not gifts bought quickly for too much money, my grandfather is the cement in this collection of people. There are never too many people for dinner; there can only be too few.

The table gets folded up and put away again until Easter and the chairs are set against the wall. Extended family members begin to show up to come and celebrate together. We get to pull the homemade cookies and candies off of the tree, my great aunts show up with their best baking… and homemade wine. Little kids and babies are passed hand to hand because there is no room on the floor, music starts, toes tap, the wine and beer flow. Small children bounce on the shoulders of someone that they are related to. I dance standing on my grandfather's shoes. This is what is important, this is family, and this is Christmas.

P.S. From our family to all of you, we wish you a Merry Christmas and a Happy New Year. 2012 will be the best yet!

FORT GOOD HOPE

Light After the Dark

Happy New Year's begins with a BANG, followed by a succession of sharp cracks as the clip is emptied on the 330 rifle.

Neighbours to the left of the first burst of rifle shots begin to empty their gun chambers skyward as well. Do you remember this? This is Canadian tradition! In the cold black night, the sound is magnified. We all hope that Uncle Ed has his rifle pointed in the right direction; he's been snipping bits of brew. Funny, he has been shooting at the Big White Moon on New Years for 70 years and has not hurt himself yet.

Aurora Borealis, the northern lights shimmer and sway with vibration of the rifle fire. Last year the boys shot up old Ron's outhouse. It's New Year's in the North. Happy New Year's, Happy New Year's! Everyone is shaking hands and smiling, it is a new beginning, a fresh start and the very best of all...the days will now begin to lengthen into the light of the midnight sun and the brightness of spring. Darkness in a northern winter grows heavy.

John Kostelnik JR. leaning on the stick beside Angelina Rabesca with her little sister Cecelia in front of her, the White Girl, Rollie Codzie with his sister Helen to the left. Joel Kostelnik approaching the group from above, the sticks are to ward off dogs.

Another form of light has begun to shine in our little village. We have a new priest, Father Rene' Fumoleau has returned to Fort Good Hope. This is a small native village of 350 people; it is located along the banks of the Mackenzie River in the

N.W.T. of Canada. Father Fumoleau held this parish in 1953, which is before my time.

The church had been a focal point for every facet of my life in the past; the previous priest had not allowed a 10-year-old girl under the same roof as "him". I had dared to ask why the Catholic Churches in Mexico could not sell some of their gold to feed the poor people and starving children that lived there. According to him this was not acceptable behavior, how dare I question the Church, how dare I ask. "Well," I replied, " those kids are starving, you said so yourself when you were asking people in Good Hope for money for them." "They look to me like they need food today." He physically threw me out of rectory.

Not being able to access this avenue of social life had left a vacancy in my life that was unrealized until Father Fumoleau arrived. There is little in the way of stimulation outside of school and school really wasn't a challenge. In the depth of winter, with terrible cold temperatures of -35 to-40 for weeks on end, an hour of sliding on the hills or snowshoeing was often on the inside edge to freezing feet and fingers or worse, lungs.

No television, no electronic gadgets, there was the odd drum or fiddle dance, I read everything from Archie comics (20 times, we only have two of them) to Darwin's Theory of Evolution, really, what a tough go. I have attempted to read it again recently and the struggle remains. How in the hell can you stay awake, to stay focused on that book? I had to have been totally desperate to attempt it at age 10.

Our Lady of Good Hope Catholic Church built between 1865 and 1885. A Canadian National Historic Site

Once again the rectory becomes a happy place. We visit Father Fumoleau to learn and play. There is no domestic help for the father so my blood sister Angelina, her cousin Dora Kelly and myself keep god and Father Fumoleau's house clean. We wash the floors, wash the dishes and keep the Chapel organized. Angelina and I serve mass in this Chapel.

Girls serving mass caused grief for Father Fumoleau. He believes that the girls should be able to serve mass in the church as well as the boys. But the guys with the rules, rule that women, even young ones have no place serving god in his house.

Women can scrub the floors, but we can't do the flashy stuff. Angel and I continue to serve mass in the chapel. We like to help; it feels good to be helping. Why would the Bishops and the Pope not like us to do this? We are only young girls, why are they so afraid of girls?

In the middle of the winter we boil what is left of the moldy potatoes for the Father, dip his eggs in oil and rotate them to try to make them last through 'til spring. Eggs develop an air pocket at the top of the shell; when you rotate eggs this keeps the shell moist and closes off the chance of air seep-age and spoilage. Six-month-old eggs smell bad; the option is dried egg, which is worse.

The boiled potatoes were cut up and fried with re-hydrated dried onion. I cannot remember Father Fumoleau eating anything else. Even as a girl, I marveled at how a person could survive by eating only fried potatoes and onions, with the occasional egg. He is in his eighties today so what can I say?

Father Fumoleau is a name well known in the North, both as a past priest and as a photographer. I am privileged to have spent time with him and to know him still. His works include the 1975 publication, AS LONG AS THE LAND SHALL LAST, he has directed two films. In November 2010 he released his fifth book, WAY DOWN NORTH. This book contains more than 100 photos from the early 1960's through to the 1990's. The photos range from the Mackenzie River to Fort Franklin and down to Yellowknife.

I am sure if Mac's Fireweed Books in Whitehorse, Yukon doesn't currently have any copies left, they will be happy to order them for you. I have promised to send him copies of the White Girl Series, which appears in the Whitehorse Star Newspaper bi-monthly, I have failed to do so to date. This is on my list for 2013.

Rene' Fumoleau lives beyond the bonds of the Internet in the huge North West Territory of Canada. I realize how lazy I've become when it becomes too difficult to print copies of my stories, stick them in an envelope, lick and stick a stamp and drop it in the mail! Father Fumoleau (old traditions die hard, I have difficulty not calling him Father) encouraged me to write this series, stating that we are losing our history and that it needs to be documented or it will continue to be lost.

He wanted to know about my father's home movies. My Father did his own form of documentation with an 8-mm camera from the back of a dog sled and in tippy canoes on icy rivers.

My mother is currently working on her book of experiences as well. I can hardly imagine being a 27-year old woman who has an active and creative mind living with the limitations that she did. Four highly charged children, although challenging were possibly her survival. She covered for the nurses at the nursing stations when needed and has some great stories as a result.

Dora Angelina and myself, with encouragement and backing from Father Fumoleau, set up and registered a community newspaper that we called the Hare Express. The name was based on the history of the community in which the people were known as the Hareskin Indians and Freddy Kelly. Freddy was known in the sports world as the "KELLY EXPRESS."

Freddy was so quiet and shy it is hard to imagine him as a member of an Olympic Team. He cross country skied in the 1972 Olympics in Japan. Freddy was a member of Father Mouchet's famous T.E.S.T program out of Inuvik, N.W.T. He literally gave his heart to cross country skiing and died far too soon.

The Hare Express was great fun, done in the fashion of the late Edith Josie's legendary columns called HERE ARE THE NEWS, which ran in the Whitehorse Star for three decades. We did not have access to her

writing at this time, but our style was very similar, a wonderful small town style. I love Edith Josie, I know that she has left but her stories are imprinted on my mind, so to me she is still alive. My day is always brighter when I think about her stories.

Excitement is building; we have something to write about in our little paper, an important man in coming to Fort Good Hope, he is a Minister, but not the same as a priest. He is a big boss in the government, he is on his way to Inuvik and is going to stop en-route to say hello to us, his shirt is so-o-o white!

Jean Chretien, the Minister of Indian and Northern Affairs, pats us roughly on our heads and walks by. My mother offers Mrs. Chretien the use of our indoor toilet. Mrs. Chretien does not comprehend my Mother's offer; there will be few of these on this tour, and mostly no toilet paper. Maybe this is the reason for the very brief visit.

I have to say that I was not overly impressed with Mr. Chretien at the time; in his abruptness he appeared rude.

On March 17, 2003 Mr. Chretien, the then Prime Minister of Canada refused to join the U.S.A. in the invasion of Iraq. This would have sacrificed more our children, sons and daughter for another gas station to supply the very thirsty U.S. with yet more fossil fuel. His stance against being bullied into this war was one of my proudest moments as a Canadian.

We were in the U.S. at the time of Canada's refusal to participate in this war. Actual family member who now live in the U.S. dis-owned us and their home country of Canada over this decision made by Chretien. The message came through loud and clear, "If you are not with us, you are against us." It was very sad.

I have never had an appreciation of bullies. I do however have an unending admiration for people in positions of power who have the gonads to stand up for what is right, regardless of the current and popular determination of what right is on a particular day.

If you don't stand for something, you will fall for anything…more of my grandfathers quoted wisdom. In my heart and in my mind on March 17th, 2003, we were no longer the "Sheeple of Canada."

P.S. It's 2012…Give Peace a chance.

FORT GOOD HOPE

LIVING WITH PUPPIES

Puppies, puppies everywhere! Sandy, my brother John's blue and brown-eyed Siberian husky has given birth to five gorgeous pups. This is my Dad's future dog team. They are beautiful blue-eyed Siberian Huskies. The runt of the litter is called Shorty; he is an exact duplicate of his father, our wheel dog named Tippy.

Tippy is classic black with white accents and the startling blue eyes that are a trademark of the Siberian husky. Tippy is the perfect wheel dog. He is slightly smaller than our other dogs, which allows him to be positioned closest to the carryall. As a bonus he absolutely hates all dogs, this motivates him to dig in and pull. In his position closest to the sleigh, his full view for the day is the furry backsides of all of the other dogs in the team, and he wants a piece of them all.

He has a bit of the "little" dog syndrome. I swear I can hear him muttering, he snarls and growls under his breathe continually…it sounds like "yeah, just wait, one day my traces will break and I'll have a chunk of your ass, ya' think a little thing like leather straps is goin' keep me from you, just wait, I'll get ya', I'll get ya'. " He comes back off of a run more worn out from his temper and the "carrot" running in front of his eyes and inches away from his snout, than the actual physical labour of being the wheel dog. Sandy is his sweetheart and the exception to his rule.

My dad's current team is old; "the old boys" are finding it hard doing the long hauls with heavy weights and breaking trail. They are the gentle giant freighter dogs that came from Wood Buffalo National Park, they had been retired when we first got them years ago. The Old Boys will be kept around only until the pups have been trained. Once they have helped to train the pups they will have to be put down, it is a reality of life, one that none of us wants to face, especially my Dad.

Whitie is our old lead dog, he is my dog. He will go to Pauline and Andre LaCoue and become their lead dog. All three of them are elders and move slower than most, so this arrangement will work well. I am very happy because Pauline and Andre will take good care of him and he won't be shot.

Angelina and Joel outside of the house full of puppies, Dawn is inside

We have a new lead dog named Ace, he comes to us from the RCMP, they are fazing out their dog teams. He is blind in one eye, this blind eye bulges out and is a milky colour, I don't like him, he has a mean feel to him. The RCMP will now use villain-sniffing ski-doos to follow hot on the trails of crooks and criminals. Fueling these mechanical beasts on long hauls is the problem, seems like everything needs to eat something to maintain motion.

Molly, a sled dog we have inherited, has produced a batch of black pups as well. They resemble Crooked Neck, a lanky black 'wolf 'dog that we have also acquired. Crooked Neck shakes every time I throw him his fish. Wolves would come into the dog runs in town and kill the dogs, few people ever claimed to have wolf dogs. The wolves of this era seemed to prefer to eat the dogs rather than breed them. If anyone suggested that they had a wolf dog eyebrows were raised in disbelief.

Somebody has been mean to Crooked Neck; his legs shake so badly when approached that it seems he can't hold himself up. If you sit quiet with your arms around his neck he calms down. He has long legs like a wolf, but the resemblance ends there.

At this point in time we have twenty-four dogs counting all of the puppies and our strange collection of charity cases. Do you know have any idea how much food they eat?

Buck the St. Bernard is my brother Kurt's dog. He is a massive dog that has bad eyesight and a mean streak. Even with his incredibly thick coat he does not have the tenacity and common sense to survive the northern winters, he freezes into the snow and then gets pissy with us when we try to get him "unstuck". The other dogs know enough to get up and move around on occasion, this prevents them from freezing into the snow.

Cubby originates from Colville Lake, one of Father Brown's showy white Samoyeds he is my brother Joel's. He looks like his father might have been something other than purebred Samoyed; I think this is possibly why he has been given away. Very good to look at these Samoyeds, but not much use as a sled dog. Cubby's time on earth could be limited I'm thinking.

With all of these puppies to play with we have an unlimited source of entertainment. The dogs are not allowed in the house…ever. Sandy is the exception; if she has pups in the winter she has to wear an apron so her teats don't freeze. Even with the apron, when it is too cold she comes in so she doesn't freeze this tender area. In the summer however it is unheard of to have a dog in the house. We are kids after all, rules are for what?

We decide that we want to get a really good look at these babies of Molly's. Their mother Molly is not as friendly with us as Sandy is. Sandy appears glad to have baby sitters' show up on occasion, Molly may take a bite out of us, we highjack her babies.

All seven of these black babies are squirming around on my mom's clean kitchen floor. Up side down they go, fat little legs splaying wildly, we sort out males and females. They are old enough to waddle across the floor and take nips at their brothers or sisters. There is a commotion going on, kids giggling at puppies, puppies yelping at shadows in this strange place, baby growls as they slide across the waxed floor and skid into each other and…Oh, Oh. Quick, we better get them outside; one baby has pooped on mom's very shiny clean floor. When one starts they all start. Sure enough, now a two-pile pick up is required.

"Get them out, get them out… quick clean it up!" "No you clean it up it was your idea!" "No way, you said it first!" Too late, my mom comes in. "What's going on in here?" "You guys know that you are not allowed to bring dogs in the house!" It was Johnnie's idea; we always say that it was Johnnies fault; he is smaller and gets away with way more than Joel and I do. "I don't care whose idea it was, clean it up!" "No wait!" "What on earth?" "Get me the dust pan." "Oh my god, Johnny (my mom is calling for my dad now) Johnny look at this!"

This is peculiar poop, it is moving around on the shiny clean floor. What makes poop move you ask? (Do you really want to know?) My mom has a background in nursing," grab those kids." Geeze, we didn't poop on the floor, what does she want? As she is yelling for dad we are scooping the mushy moving stuff, pronto.

"I thought you wormed those dogs " she states to my dad, "well you obviously missed these puppies they are alive and crawling with worms and now we will have to de-worm the kids as well." No big deal, we all got de-wormed in the spring every year, dogs with worms, kids with worms it just works that way. (Don't think that as adults you are immune to the squirmy beings)

When there was no worm medicine in town the old people would give their dogs a penny. They said that the worms didn't like the Whiteman's money. I do believe that bugs just don't like copper and silver, which are old parasitical remedies from days gone by, that work very well. I'll tell you about the cure for an earache another time…

Let's just get this topic over with. Have you ever eaten rosehips? We would wait until a frost hit the berries to soften the pulp and let the skin slip off easily. Everyone called rosehips "itchy bum berries". I never knew if this was because they also contained worms of a sort or if swallowed, the seeds became an incredible source of roughage that caused this itch. Aren't we all glad that this particular subject has now been dealt with! And all within one story too, yahoo!

P.S. The smell of the village in the springtime from recycled dog food was horrific. As the snow melted, the land mines of poop became exposed. This was really hard on the mukluks. The deal my dad offered was a "penny a pile" on a voluntary basis or do it without being agreeable and don't get the penny. (Total blackmail) The smell of eau du dog in the springtime still gags me.

FORT GOOD HOPE

MOVING ON UP

We will be moving yet again. This move will take us to the Arctic Ocean and into the domain of the "Eaters of Raw Meat." Coppermine which is now called Kugluktuk, is located on the Coronation Gulf, this is part of the Northwest Passage. Kugluktuk means the Place of the Moving Waters.

Coppermine (Kugluktuk) is the most westerly community in the newest Territory in Canada called Nunavut. Nunavut was established on April 01, 1999. Located on the shores of the Arctic Ocean and mouth of the Copper River this village of 1,200 persons is 15 km from the "Bloody Falls". So named for a massacre from a battle that ensued between the Dene and the Inuit over hunting and fishing grounds and probably the theft of women.

Stories of the horrors that follow the ancestral enemies of the Dene are many. As actual memories dwindle, legends grow. Every culture has its "Glory Days." It was rumored that as late as 1948 a family group of Inuit had eaten the hearts of two priests. In fact two Inuit hunters, one of them a Shaman did indeed kill two Priests, whether they ate them or not I have no idea, this occurred in 1917 and is a documented crime. The two Inuit were sentenced to death, but had the death sentence overthrown because the courts decided that there was undue provocation from the priests.

Parts of people and animals were eaten as symbolic, if you wanted good eyesight, you should eat good eyes…I wonder if the Inuit of that day viewed these particular priests as having good hearts, there was no discussion about evidence leading to the consumption of cranial matter.

Angelina my blood sister in Fort Good Hope has been saving her money. This move to Coppermine may put a kink in our plans. We are going on vacation together to the outside next summer. Angelina lives in Fort Good Hope and has never been outside of her community of 350 people; she will come south with us for two months.

During the previous summer I had an accident. July 01 is sports day in the village. Competitions are held in everything from canoe racing, tug of war to running and jumping. This year I am determined to beat Tony Grandjambe and Harold Cook. I have learned to run like the wind out of necessity. Few of the girls that want to "pound" me can run really fast, but I take no chances, they seldom approach in groups of one.

I can keep in front of most of the smaller boys. I have developed a strategic deek…run like hell, let them get almost in grabbing range then drop, cover my head and let them trip over me. I get several mukluked feet to the head, but it is way better that the beating I will get if they catch me. I am little and I am fast. I will beat the boys.

With time to kill until the festivities start, I loiter downstairs in the basement swinging on the Tarzan rope that my brothers and I have tied to a beam. With a knot tied in the end of this rope it hangs three feet above the solid concrete floor. I grab the rope and take a full run that swings me up and out. The last thing I remember is hearing the wail of the siren that announces the beginning of the races.

Consciousness brings excruciating pain and dizziness. I retch over the side of the bed. Bed? I am in my parent's bed, this is serious, I have enough sense left to realize this. Raising my head from the pillow causes black spots to swim I front of me and oh no, I throw up what is left of my lunch all over myself and the bed yet again, the pain in my head is tremendous. I can't keep water in my stomach. It feels like days are drifting in and out, I can't eat and only want to sleep.

Why won't my mother just let me sleep? It is becoming serious, I need to keep something down and now my stomach hurts from throwing up so much. Trying to go to the bathroom, I can't walk…what is wrong with my legs; they won't do what I want them to do. The world is on tilt.

Mrs. McCormick, the Hudson Bay Co., mangers wife brings me a banana. It has been a very long time since I have seen a banana and three days since I have been able to keep anything in my stomach. Do you remember when things had to be in their season to be purchased? Strawberries were available in the spring, when they got ripe from the sun, and only then. They tasted just like a strawberry by the way. We had gone outside for Christmas, but bananas weren't available, it had been three years since I'd eaten a banana.

This banana came from Mrs. McCormick's private stash; they weren't for sale in the HBC for sure. Mrs. McCormick used to tell me stories about their vacations in Mexico with an intense longing in her voice. This elderly couple travels to Mexico in the 1960's for their holidays.

I am cautious: I will be thoroughly pissed off at myself if I puke this up! It is a wonderful banana. Creamy, smooth and sweet, I take tiny little nibbles and savour every one. Please don't come back up, please…it just doesn't taste as good coming backwards. I am on the road to recovery, the banana stays put, now a little water…little by little I gain my equilibrium, to this day I get dizzy spells.

There is no doctor; my mom is the current nurse. At the end of the summer two Doctors are kayaking up the mighty Mackenzie. My dad takes me down the riverbank to see them. They look in my eyes and shine a portable flashlight to see if my pupils respond. With strong fingers one of them feels my head, he stops and starts a few time. "Hm-m-m," he says," do you have trouble with your balance?" he asks me, "not anymore, just if I get really tired, but then it goes away." He tells my dad that he doesn't believe that there is any brain damage, but that he thinks I have fractured my skull.

The nearest hospital is in Yellowknife, which is 805 kilometers by air. They would have to call an airplane in to do a Mercy flight, a Mercy Flight is when a pilot flies through white outs and totally illogical situations to try to save someone life. A mercy flight to Fort Good Hope on July 01 would have been easy in their books. However, by the time that they got there, if I was going to die from the bang on my head I would be dead and that's just how it is sometimes…I didn't die and I still maintain some mental function.

Devastation sets in, another move. It has taken me so long to establish myself in the pecking order of this community, and now I will have to start all over again. A little White Girl with an Indian accent arriving in the land of the eaters of raw meat wearing my beautiful red "parkie" that shouts "hey, I'm from Fort Good Hope," one of your ancestral and sworn enemies.

I will have to leave Angelina, how can I live without my sister? I am twelve years old now, and the girls that I will have to fight will be bigger, how do you fight with someone who eats raw meat? I have a few months to get used to the idea, At night I have wild dreams about banquets of raw meat and beating drums.

My mom is excited, her and my father have received an invitation to attend the

1st Annual R.C.M.P. Ball in Inuvik N.W.T. Inuvik is officially 11 years old at this time. My parents will fly on the R.C.M.P plane with Bob and Lois Anderson. Bob Anderson is the law in Fort Good Hope, he is very big, and he is the R.C.M.P.

They have three little kids, Donna Lynn, Lisa and Robert Jr. Robert Jr. is legendary, he pulled the pin on the fire extinguisher in his dad's office (which is attached to the house) and sprayed all of the official papers with foam. Robert Jr. is just a baby. We are amazed at how much trouble you can cause when you are only two years old and you can get away with it!

P.S. Bob and Lois Anderson lived for years as the law in Watson Lake in the Yukon Territory. Karen Lang forwards the Whitehorse Star with the White Girl Series to them in Alberta where they have retired. I would like to say hello to them and wish them well.

COPPERMINE, N.W.T.

(Kugluktuk)

Coppermine is a small Eskimo village located at the confluence of the Copper River and the pebbled shores of the crystal clear Arctic Ocean. As the bird flies south to Yellowknife N.W.T it is about 540 miles and from Coppermine to Edmonton, Alberta, flying with the same bird, it is 860 miles.

At the time of these stories the population of Coppermine was approximately 1,200 persons. Most of the people were Eskimo (Inuit) with a few Kabloonah (whiteyes) employed by the Canadian Government and the Hudson Bay Company.

Can you imagine living on the Edge of World with the Eskimos? I did, these are great stories, the people are real people, and with real names I have only changed names in one storey because I thought that I should. Most people in these stories are alive today. I would like to say hello to them. Hello all of my friends, hi Grace and Allen and all of Allen's sisters oh yes and Helen, I wish you well.

Sincerely
Dawn, the white girl

COPPERMINE

THE EDGE OF THE WORLD

April in the Arctic means there are still three months left until spring arrives. Spring, springs into action overnight and the next day it is summer. And then, just before you realize that it is summer, snow flies and you skip over the season of fall and fast-forward back into winter once again.

But in April you get to squint into the sun. It blinds you with its prisms of brilliance. Snow banks transform into mountains of diamonds that humans cannot capture in their too warm fingers. Dazzling white snow is defined by the deepest of blue skies. A blaze of sunlight that doesn't last for hours yet, but it is enough to revitalize the solar powered smiles on people's faces.

Hearts sing in the sunshine after months of darkness. Cold remains, but the smiles threaten to deplete it with their radiance of warmth.

Our house is buried in a snow bank. We have just arrived in Coppermine, N.W.T., moving here from Fort Good Hope in the same territory of Canada's north. Even in my grief at being wrenched from my blood sister Angelina and having to leave my home and many, many friends, I am in awe that we have to climb down a snowdrift to get into our new house.

Tomorrow they will dig out the doorway so we can move our belongings in, but for today, we climb up the hard, snow swept bank that has drifted and covered in the entry to our home. We slide; fall down into the doorway and through the door.

This house is a rectangle with an L-shaped hallway that separates the bedrooms and bathroom from the main living area. The kitchen and casual dining are separated by a diesel-burning oil furnace located plainly in sight, right in the centre of the house…a little closer to the kitchen. By the kitchen at the end of the living room there is a dining area as well.

Diesel fuel is the smell that colours this home. Partitions that separate the hallway to the bedrooms and bath from the rest of the house, do not reach either the floor or the ceiling by one foot along the full perimeter. The space above and below the wall is needed to allow the heat to circulate in this extreme climate. There is no forced air system on our diesel stove; heat is moved by convection only.

I have saved the worst for last; the most dreaded thing in the world... there is no flush toilet! We must use the infamous "honey bucket". I notice that my mom is not real happy about this either. So what can you do if you have to pooh? Outside behind the snow bank is an even worse option.

There are no outhouses here and most certainly no trees to hide behind. Consequently, everyone lives with the bucket. A honey bucket is a large can with a toilet seat and lid. The can is lined with the equivalent to an extra-strength green plastic garbage bag. Pine Sol cleaner is used to disguise the eau due turd, it does not!

When the bag is full, you remove it and replace it with a new bag. It is just lovely, perching above the full bag that no one wants to take out until they absolutely have to. Said green bag is thrown outside of the house and left to freeze. The honey wagon comes along to pick it up once a week.

You don't want to hear what happens next, but this is reality, this is what really happened. Frozen honey bags are taken out and left on the sea ice to await spring break-up. From here they will get carried out to sea with the ice and drop their load into the pristine Arctic Ocean. This happened a long time ago, before people knew better.

I think that Victoria, B.C., does something similar in this day. There is not as much of a visual impact when raw sewage is run directly from this Capital City in Beautiful British Columbia, Canada, onto the floor of the Ocean. But given the size of their population, the ability for production of this product would have much greater impact on this undersea garden where their food grows. I have heard that fish and mollusks from this area are flavoured differently from less populated areas that don't pump raw poop into their food production area.

Coppermine had a population of 1,200 when this memory was created. Not as much poop production as Victoria, and by the way since we are on the topic; has Dawson City, Yukon finally got its poop together and quit pumping crap into the Legendary Yukon River?

Once upon a time in Coppermine a rookie with immense possibilities joined the honey bucket brigade. His heart was in the right place. He diligently heaved the frozen piles of green encased turds onto the wagon and carried them out onto the sea ice.

He is prompt; he leaves not a green plastic turd carrier anywhere. They have been known to try to escape, these slippery green bags. The dogs find them and all hell and smell breaks loose. In the spring the lost ones thaw and can be tracked down, by cautiously approaching from down wind, they cannot seep unnoticed. (At this point no one wants to be the one who finds it and has to dispose of it). With his enthusiasm and in his innocence he forgets one very important step in the elimination of elimination.

Sea ice moves and shifts and heaves, especially along the shoreline. With the influence of the Copper River running along the foreshore of the village, the sea ice would swirl and back eddy in front of the community with the current from the river.

The sea ice is gone but the green garbage type bags swim in front of the village and do a full 360 and return yet again and again; around and around they go. This is very unusual behavior for the green guys, what is going on? Ah-h-h …out come the guns; bodies crouch, stand tall or lay on their stomach's, rifles cradled up to shoulders, men, women, boys and girls. The beach has become a shooting gallery complete with carnival atmosphere.

Huge smiles and cheers are heard as a strike is made. Favorites are chosen; people clap when a good shot is made. This is more fun than hunting seals, much easier for sure. Bang, poof, bang, poof…the floating green islands of poop drop their cargo as they are shot full of holes. Feeding the fishes is an old divers expression that comes to mind for some reason.

Experienced Honey Jockeys know they have to puncture the honey bags or they float and remain floating on the surface of the sea, shameful, for the entire world to see. A knife if carried by the "pros", they give the bags a quick jab before they are left out on the sea ice.

As a species, our favourite form of garbage disposal has been to throw stuff into our water systems. If we don't see it, it is obviously gone…brilliance! Now we get to drink our garbage, eat our garbage and bathe our babies in it too. Next we add deadly toxins to fix our mistakes, disguising garbage with poisonous chemicals is an amazing move. What can I say? Watching honey bucket bags getting shot when I was eleven years old was fun, we are much older now, we know better.

I have gotten ahead of myself; we need to back up to snowdrifts and winter and brand new town. Our house sits across the road from this pristine ocean. An endless expanse of white and ice is our front yard; the back yard is endless white as well. I look out to sea and see what? I think I could be standing on the edge of the world. A curve at the horizon is apparent, where are the trees? I understand the concept of walking off the edge of the earth; I can see the slightly curved end of it.

How do these people set snares with no trees? My new school sits on top of one of the many rounded rock hills that form slight definitions in the endless miles that make up our backyard. Our house is sitting on some type of pillar off of the ground. Weird, one side of the house is wrapped and banked in snow; the other side is barren and rocky.

Black is the contrast in the never-ending white. Further up past the school I can see many boxy houses; there is not a lot of colour from where I stand. Rounded rocks on the hills have been swept clean of snow and show faces of black smooth stone.

Even the snow is strange. I can walk anywhere that I like and not sink up to my knees. Snowshoes would be useless here. Snow banks and the snow in general are had and windswept. The Bombardier, with all of its weight barely dents the surface of the snow.

Blocks of snow are carved easily with a long knife and stacked to create porches in front of doorways that act as Arctic entries to keep snow and wind out of houses. These porches also allow you to dig your way out if you are buried after a whiteout. You can break through a snow porch and get out.

People begin to arrive up to welcome us. Everyone shakes hands and smiles…lots! I am nervous, who can smile that much? My red Indian "parkie" creates a stir and a crowd of young girls forms around me. There is much touching and patting of my red stroud parkie, they trace the embroidered flowers with many fingers, I am not liking this.

Ow! What was that? Again, I feel the sting. It feels like a really bad bee sting. I look into the faces that are way too close to my face; there is no change in any of the expressions that are up close and too personal.

Again, the bee bites, I don't flinch this time. Again, they bite and again. I stare right back, so this is how it will be.

The strange sounding chatter dies down and the girls begin to back away. I can't understand what they are saying, but I know that the next few months are going to be rough ones. When I undress that night, I have little black bruises covering my arms and legs where I have been pinched.

P.S. how can a northern story be told without having a discussion about honey buckets? Outhouses could not be dug this far north in the permafrost if you could find dirt, the rock is obviously too hard. So hail the bucket!

While under construction the year before last, the Captain installed an indoor toilet for me on Valentine's Day...do you remember what you got on Valentines Day two years ago? It was a cold year that year, I was very happy and I remember it still.

COPPERMINE

FROM INDIANS TO ESKIMOS

Out with the old and slide into the new. My two brothers and I stand shivering at the school door. Winds howl off of the snow swept rock that stands guard above the school. Willy wags wing gusts of powered snow into the corner that we huddle. Frigid fingers tear and tug at our faces and pull on our clothing. Powdered snow clings to our stroud Indian "parkies."

The school bell rings but the door refuses to budge. One more pull on the door, our very best attempt, still no movement. We can hear voices laughing and calling in the distance, how in the hell do you get into this place? We cannot figure it out, but this is perfect, we can go home. We have done all that we can to access what we really don't want entry to anyway, a new school at almost the end of the school year, it just doesn't get any worse than this!

Yes it does. We arrive at the door to our new school clad in the clothing of the Inuit's traditional enemies, the Dene Indians of the McKenzie River in the N.W.T. of Canada. From experience we know that it's not good to be different.

It is April in the High Arctic. We have just moved to Coppermine which is in the N.W.T at this time, it is now located in Nunavut, Canada's newest northern territory. The year is 1969.

In three days, we have gone from living in the Boreal Forests, which are home to the Dene of Fort Good Hope to the High Arctic tundra, the hunting grounds of the once nomadic Inuit. Coppermine has a population of 1,200. There is a mix of families here.

School goes all the way to grade seven in Coppermine. If there are enough students and a teacher is available, grade eight will be offered next year as well. This year there is grade seven. Had we stayed in Good Hope I would have to leave and stay in a hostel to attend public school this fall in either Grollier Hall in Inuvik or Akaitcho Hall in Yellowknife. Classes only went to Grade 6 in Fort Good Hope.

Our move to Coppermine was not pre-determined by our schooling. If there were no classes we would have to go with the other kids to the hostels. There was a government policy that they did not want White people in their employment to stay more than two years in one community; people got too attached and became native if they stayed too long in one place. We had spent more than two years in Fort Good Hope; we were way behind in their schedule.

This is enough effort, knock, knock, knocking on the door…we begin to sneak back towards home. "Oh, there you are!" "Someone thought they saw you at the emergency exit." "Come along now." Mr. Adams, with a British accent that complements his definite headmaster attitude, will be my teacher. He puts up with no nonsense and has directed us directly to where we should be going.

My brothers are sent to their new classes respectively. With his hand on my back, Mr. Adams propels me into the class and announces, "This is a new student, her name is Dawn." "I expect that you will make her welcome to our class." I raise my eyes slowly from the floor and cautiously look around the room trying not to make direct eye contact.

WOW: there is an assortment of kids in here. Eskimo kids and white kids all mixed up, some are looking directly at me and are smiling. Their eyes are smiling as well, not just their mouths. I notice a few of the "pinchers" in the class, but there are only a few. Holy, this class is bigger than our wh-o-l-e-e school in Fort Good Hope. I mean the whole school, from beginners to grade six. There is only grade six and seven in this class.

I had encountered the "pinchers" when people came to welcome us to our new home and community two days before. While shaking my hand and smiling at me en masse, some of the welcoming committee had managed to inflict more than a few biting pinches. These had left my arms and legs covered in little black bruises.

I had refused to acknowledge the attack, knowing that this is a challenge to find out exactly what kind of stuff I am made of. Sneaky mean little bullies. The pinches get harder and harder without any response from me. I stand my ground; they can't grab handfuls of my skin without being noticed. I look them all right in the eye, now they are afraid, they don't know what to make of me, this is good.

What are a few biting pinches that leave little black marks compared to the bloody noses and beatings that I'd had in the past? This is disconcerting to me however. The people on the McKenzie River were direct. There was no way that they would smile and pinch, they would walk right up to your face and tell you that they didn't like you…it could then turn into a bloody nose, but you knew where you stood. I can tell you that the double talk of white society still baffles me.

Why would anyone say one thing and do another? This is very strange. There is no honour in this duplicity. How can you ever know who your friends are?

There are brown kids and white kids and ivory kids in this class. I am no longer the only white girl. The relief of this is overwhelming. I am not the only one who is different here. I will not stand out because I am white, maybe because I am mouthy and a 'proudy', but not because I am white. I will be judged by who I am, not by the colour of my skin!

I had no idea that there would be more like me in this place, I am so happy, I smile back tentatively. I am directed to my seat at the front of the class; Mr. Adams wants to keep an eye on the new student. For once I am not at the front of the class because of my lack of height, among the Eskimo girls I am almost a giant, they are short statured.

This is fun, there are incredible pictures that the students have crafted adorning the walls, along the shelves at the side of the class, soapstone carvings are on display, the work of these young student artists.

I learn the Inuit word for Coppermine is "Kugluktuk"; we are all being taught the written language of the Inuktitut, which is a syllabary style of writing. The Northwest Territories government had a true type font developed for it called Pigiamiq. The little triangles are easy to learn, I think…much easier than the spoken word for me. I had become proficient in the Slavey language, which sings a soft song.

The language of Inuinnaqtun blankets the sub-dialect of Kangiryuarmiutan (the language spoken in Coppermine) and is guttural to me. It's spoken in your throat it sounds to me, more than on your tongue. I have difficulty with pronunciation and don't learn to speak this language very well. I may have managed more proficiency if I had started to learn this younger or had been more self-assured.

Embarrassment is the destruction of puberty and adolescents, they are embarrassed about everything. Have you as parents noticed this?

I love the written words of Kangiryuarmiutat. I wish I had been more mature in my approach to the language.

A classroom has been converted for use as a gym. There is limited ceiling height, so no basketball. The one big window in this room has been covered with heavy wire mesh to allow us to play floor hockey, soccer, limited volleyball and the game of choice, dodge ball.

Dodge ball is the passion! Grade seven students range in age from 13 to 17 years of age. School did not start for some for the kids who lived off of the land until they were six to ten years old. English is a second language for the Eskimo kids; most of them don't learn it until they attend grade beginners. Can you imagine the culture shock? Actual levels of grading were based on kids ability to "read like a white man and to write like a white man."

My mother has my brother Kurt's beginner's report card. It still makes us laugh to see this crazy grading system. After growing up on the McKenzie River, I am not sure that my baby brother didn't have almost the same challenge of reading and writing like a white man as the other kids did. I can't remember if he passed this level or not. I know that he hated school with a passion and would run away and hide; he was only five at the time.

Teams for dodge ball are picked; to my surprise I am included in the draft. I swear that ball was travelling towards Philips head at 100m.p.h.! In traditional Inuk style, this is a game of strength and/or endurance. I am fast; I determine it is better to dodge this death missile than try to catch it.

Elizabeth, an older girl, leans into the ball and lets it slam into her chest; her arms instinctively clutch the ball. Ah-h-h comes unbidden from the mouths of her opposition. They all crowd in fear in the corners, awaiting repercussion. She will redirect the ball toward us now. I appreciate that she is not picking on me, she has her eye on one of the older boys, he watches her warily.

Slam! The ball crashed into his chest and now he is heading back for Elizabeth, a friendly little game of who can take off whose head. A bell rings and we head back to class, I think my head has been saved by the bell, thank you, thank you. Class is over for the day.

Outside everyone waits to se the new kids. I am shy, unused to being

see

in such a crowd of curious and friendly kids. Crowds were never good were I came from. It turns out that I am a sea kid, the town kids live up above the school, there are very few of us that live down by the sea.

Torn pieces of cardboard litter the schoolyard. Town kids slide down the hill to school on these tatters; they leave them, as they have to climb the hill home. My new friend Grace Elgok grabs a brown paper remnant and motions for me to do the same. Basic form of recycling, when you don't have much, you find multiple uses for what you do have.

We step over the bank together, place the bit of cardboard under our butts and slide down toward the frozen ocean and our homes.

P.S. A most happy surprise, Mrs. Grace Priest whom I first met in Fort Norman as a missionary had moved to Coppermine to shepherd the Eskimos. She has been very good to me. I do appreciate her, we cross paths once again.

Coppermine

NORTHERN GAMES

April is a grand month for sliding. Sunshine warms the surface of the snow and ice glazes road surfaces and drifts of snow that have banked up during the long winter of whiteouts. There is no such thing as a fall season when you live without trees that have leaves to fall, there is freeze up.

Boats and some motors (also known in the north as kickers) are hauled up on the pebble beach of the Arctic Ocean at this freeze up time and left for spring thaw out time. For everything there is a time and a season.

I have seen boats being hauled on Komatiks in the spring when there is danger of falling through the ice. A Komatik is a sled that is pulled behind the Ski-doo with a 12 to 20 foot lead line. A person could survive by at least jumping into the boat tied onto the sled if your Ski-doo breaks through the sea ice.

There is a minimal tide on this frozen coast. Humps of hulls are apparent under the snow and god help whoever did not remove their kicker and properly put it to bed for the winter, somewhere else. A kicker cover is the perfect apparatus for sliding down anything! Hills with rocks and ice and of course, the school steps.

Being dragged behind a Ski-doo with your butt stuck in one of these lids doing 20 M.P.H. without control is the absolute most fun! With kid-sized butts being a perfect fit in these "borrowed" caps, we scrabble back up the hills imitating hermit crabs on southern beaches. There are only a few of these gems to be had. If we unattached our backsides for a second, it will become someone else's property.

Those pitiful kids without kicker caps are left to carry around pieces of waxy cardboard to slide with. The cardboard chunks offer no protection from rocks and other sharp objects. The cardboard gets smaller and smaller…

Snow blindness is real; there are no sunglasses to be had. We are a motley crew with our butts stuck in kicker covers and eyes covered in wrap-around hand carved goggles known in Inuktitut as ggaak. Styles of ggaak vary according to the carver and the piece of wood that chance has provided high above the tree line.

My cool shades are two separate pieces of wood, round and of a size that they fit perfectly over my eyes and nestle into my eye sockets. Slits have been cut into these oval pods to allow for sight. The two eye pods are connected across my nose with leather caribou thong. The ties that go around my head and are tied in the back are also leather thongs. They stretch if they get wet.

Other kids model goggles that are single units which have been carved in one continual piece that covers both eyes and fits over their nose, again tied in the back of their head with a leather thong. This is truly designer eyewear, every set is an original designed by every person that carves them. There are no two alike, it suits our personalities, who wants of be like everyone else?

April is also the month that a large percentage of the community spreads out on to the sea ice for the spring seal hunt. I have not gone out on a hunt yet. kids are let out to participate and help on this hunt.

Kids return to class after a week of sealing as adults, with white circles around their eyes and black peeling skin on their cheeks, chins and nosed. Inuit have fairer complexions than the Dene on the McKenzie Rive. Spring sunshine gets magnified and reverberates off of millions of snow crystals, these people are getting sunburned and frost bitten at the same time.

The black peeling marks on faces are from frostbite or maybe a solid freezing. This happens when your face is exposed above the shield on the Ski-doo or you were facing into the wind on the Komatik. Protection from the wooden goggles prevents the area around the eyes from getting sunburned or tanned.

Games that Inuit play do not require much space or equipment. There was neither of these to be had when you lived a nomadic life and existed in micro-confined areas during the winter. Snow houses known to most everyone as igloos were lived in during the winter months. Small confined spaces needed less to heat; these people were "green" before there was a green.

Hides of caribou and seals covered supporting bits of precious wood or big bones of large sea mammals as shelter in the short time when the snow is gone, the summer cottage. Living without wood to construct shelter and burn to cook or heat your home takes much ingenuity. During the short months of summer there is little need or time for games.

In the summer the world is awake and begging to be explored. The whole family, including the very smallest of children has to contribute to gathering and harvesting fat seals, caribou and berries to carry themselves through the next endless night of winter. There is barely enough time for so many projects that have to be done under a sun that circles endlessly for a month. The endless night of winter is when people cooped up in a confined space need to entertain themselves; the Inuit were masters at this.

Their physical games hinged mainly on brute strength and endurance. A thong of caribou has a multitude of uses. It can keep your kamiks (shoes) on and prevent you mitts from being lost. Or it can be used to rip off your opponent's ear in a game of tug of war.

This is a simple concept. Loop the leather thong over your ear and your competitor's ear, then with all of the strength in you neck and head, pull back until your competition yells the Inuit equivalent of "uncle." Warning, this may not happen until there is a show of blood. Sometimes the thong slips. Everyone laughs and slaps each other on the back. There is a tie; no one wants to have to feel bad for the losers.

Another deadly challenge comes in the shape of a wooden dart shaped as a teardrop. A narrow end fits into your hand; the bottom of the teardrop has been fitted with a nail that has been sharpened to a fine and deadly point. The object of the game is to place your hand flat and out and very vulnerable on the table…all of you tender fingers are spread wide.

You then throw the dart and try to stick it between your fingers. Of course you don't want to stick it into your hand, the object is NOT to stick it in your hand silly! This dart has to be thrown HARD in order to make it stick into the table or it does not court.

It really, really hurts if the dart jabs into your hand. If your throw is disqualified, your opposition gets to take a turn at the throw. They can throw the dart at your hand! You hope they like you, you hope they are good shots and you really hope that you have the guts to not move your hand as the throw is made. An Eskimo version of chicken!

We played games that are now and integral part of the Arctic Winter Games, the last time that I checked anyway. The one leg kick with variations is still tough to accomplish. The following is an old endurance and strength game I have not seen or heard of for many, many years.

You kneel with your hands behind your back and remain upright. A friend can sit on your legs or you can tuck them under something that will support your weight. You then bend forward with you hands behind your straight back. Get your face close enough to the floor to pick up a small object that has been place out there, with your teeth. You then lengthen out your body and replace the object just beyond where you found it.

You return your body to its upright position, with your hands still behind your back. You can't fall or you are disqualified, try it, I dare you. Your opponent repeats this procedure and attempts to move the object further than you just did. We used a tiny hand made seal as the object and our mascot.

I have seen persons in positions of impossibility while attempting this feat. Of course if you were not physically inclined there are always games of cards, a favourite is crib.

P.S. In 1972 I came south from Inuvik with the McKenzie Delta Drum Dancers to participate in a cultural competition for the Arctic Winter Games. We won Gold Ulus for our performances.

Whitehorse is a wondrous City for us kids from the north. Wow, there are so many people! Look at all of the cars, such food, so much excitement. The people of Whitehorse were so very kind, smiling when we walked out into the street forgetting such things as cars...we have no cars were we live.

When we blocked the sidewalks because there were no sidewalks where we live, people walked around us and smiled at our awe, we did not know how the customs worked. That was 40 years ago.

I am proud to say that the people of Whitehorse still maintain their open-

hearted hospitality. They realize that visitors to our Territory come from different cultures and countries. Everyone goes out of their way to make our very special visitors feel at home. Have a most wonderful time at this Arctic Winter Games and remember, THERE IS NO SWEAT IN THE ARCTIC!

COPPERMINE

WHAT'S IN A NAME

On the Mackenzie River there were apparent cultural influences from the Hudson Bay Company and French Voyagers, to the men who had worked on the barges and plied the great river looking for adventure, fame and fortune. Seeking gold and the money that the fur trade offered lured people from every walk of life.

From Grandambe to Yakeleya, and Cooks to Kakfwis and Norwegians and Gaudets, the river flows with cultural combinations. Masuzumis are purported to be part of a family of Samurai's from Japan. There were rumours of a Samurai sword in personal possession in Fort Good Hope, a fascinating history. I first met Michael Jackson when he was born in the late 1960's in Fort Good Hope, N.W.T., son of Wilfred and Lucy Jackson. Rocky Norwegian had blond hair and pale eyelashes as I recall. There are Lennies and Yallees and Barnaby's...

In Coppermine the flavour is distinctly different. Influenced once again by adventurers and with a slight twist, whalers. Now we have Niptanatiaks, Omingmuks, Kayoganas and Klengenbergs. I do apologize for any names that I have miss-spelled throughout this storey; it has been a few years since I have rolled some of these off of my tongue. Jimmy Niptanatiak worked with my father.

Jimmy's son Alan and daughter Mary Ann became our fast friends. Mary Ann was a little doll in her itigi (parka) the word that I remember for parka. Everyone refers to them as the "Nips", way faster. I have just found out that 36 years ago my friend Grace Elgok married my friend Allen Nip.

Religion is much more relaxed on the coast. We attend the Catholic Church with the Nips and the Elgoks; there are few Catholic Eskimo families. There are many differences here. Life has been easier; I don't have to fight my way to and from school everyday. I have met lots of girls who want to be friends. When you don't have to fight you can learn all kinds of new things.

We play Ping-Pong at the Anglican rectory with John and Angela Sperry. Mrs. Priest teaches girl guides every Wednesday night at the community centre. There are shows at the Community Center every Saturday for .10 cents and its .25 cents for an ice cream. Can you imagine, the show is different every week!

I babysit for Diane and Richard Gau. They have a little boy baby named Jeffery. We go to the show together. I love to watch him; he is such a good boy. When he goes to sleep I am allowed to play records. Mr. & Mrs. Gau are members of Columbia Record Club, they have an incredible collection of music…and they have books!

It was an easy time of acceptance as a child. We played cowboys and Eskimos until it was way too late, our biggest challenge was to be able to pull start the skidoo. If you could start it, you could use it. No keys, muscle powered starter and in the cold it was tough. We would try with two kids to pull the cord on the skidoo, almost impossible with us ending up on top of each other, laughing like idiots.

In the "yard" by our house was the warehouse and garage. The warehouse stored excess rations (food supplies). The garage was exactly what it sounds like. On the River we ordered food that arrived by barge once a year. On the Sea we ordered food that arrived by ship during the open water season. A difference in food orders was that my mom would make out her own list of case goods etc. and have it shipped up the Mackenzie River by barge, in Coppermine she had to order by A, B or C army type ration.

A ration was a combination of food supplies that was determined necessary and nutritious for survival by the Canadian Military. In the warehouse were numerous cases of jam, canned wieners and canned potatoes. Lots of the left overs were things that no one wanted to eat. By having to order rations A, B or C you could not get what you wanted or needed but this gave you what the government determined you should have…sounds familiar?

Who by choice eats canned wieners? I can hear the ration gnomes from the south determining that, "those people in the north at the end of the world should appreciate that they are getting good, civilized food, it is much healthier for them." "It has to be way better than anything that they can get locally!" You should have seen the Arctic Char that came wild from the Coppermine River!

We had water delivery to our homes. Water tanks are located in heated porches. Kids have wonderful imaginations, which need to be cultivated. Intelligent minds require stimulation and if its not readily available they will create their own amusement. It can be good stimulation, it can be bad and it can be just plain hilarious.

In the warehouse was case upon case of Tang. Tang is powdered orange flavoured sugar crystals that are made into "juice". Orange and the wondrous new grapefruit tang which was popular with the adults but not particularly with the kids must have been considered essential because the rations came with an abundance of it.

My brothers were young boys with great imaginations. It is too much temptation to have a tanker truck full of water sitting beside a warehouse full of tang. How could you not want to make a tanker full of tang? They howled with laughter imagining the expressions on people's faces when tang flowed through the taps. What would it be like having a tang bath? Tang flavoured oatmeal could be good…unfortunately; they were caught in the act of creating juice.

I wish that they had succeeded; we in the north would still talk and laugh about it, as it is this storey is legend. They had managed to dump several cases of the tang into the tanker truck before they were caught and disbanded. The Tang Gang.

Keeping active minds busy with limited resources is difficult in long months of dark. I am a reader. I read everything that I can find; I get into trouble for reading too much. Can you imagine my excitement when an author of one of the books that I had read was coming to Coppermine to do research for another book! This is good. He would be staying at the Hudson Bay staff house. That was bad.

Under threat of death most young girls were told to stay a hundred miles away from the Hudson Bay staff house. I developed a friendship with Shawna; her father was the manager of the Hudson Bay. She was also under threat of death if she went near the staff house; she was an avid reader as well. Shawna had also read this authors books about life where we lived. Although the stories seemed a bit far-fetched to those of us that lived here, we imagined that the people outside (in the south) would be pretty excited by this authors books.

A couple of cases of whiskey are smuggled into a dry northern community, cheap research. Men arrive at the staff house under cover of dark to sip whiskey with this writer from the south. Some remember him from the last time he came to do " research". Whiskey flows and the words begin to flow faster than the whiskey does.

"In old times when caribou don't come and seals played below with the sea god Sedna, we eat lemmings!" "Not too-o bad you know, little bones get caught in your throat." "Lemming and Aqiggiq (ptarmigan) soup makes you strong!" "One swallow for those guys and its a-l-l-l gone." "Even them little bones." The more whiskey that flowed the more colourful the stories became.

Did I let that out? I must have been in the room to hear that. Shawna and I decide that the risk is worth our lives to set eyes on this famous Canadian author. We stand close to the door and access to quick escape; the light is dim in the crowd of people that fills the room.

Sitting at the head of the Government Issue red maple table is a little man with a big beard he has pen in hand and is intent on writing down the musings of drunken beings. Everyone laughs as they try to out do each other's tall tales.

Whiskey breath in my face, "you know what we call that guy?" the face behind the alcohol fumes commands. "Of course I know what he is called," I retort with 12-year-old disgust. "No, you know what we call that guy?" 100 proof breath asks again. "Fine, fine, what do you call that guy?" "That's Hardly Know it," he giggles.

P.S. My Dad would have throttled me if he had known that I had gone to the Hudson's Bay Staff house, he will know now. It's my dad's (John Kostelnik) birthday on March 27th, Happy Birthday Dad, we both survived me!

COPPERMINE

EASTER IN THE ARCTIC

Please, please, please, can I? Please let me go, I will be careful, I'll dress warm and I'll listen.

My friend Alice as I will call her for this storey, is going out for the Easter weekend on the sea ice. Her family is travelling with two skidoos and two Komatiks to hunt seals on the long weekend; I have been invited to come along. This would be my first experience of hunting /camping on the frozen Ocean with no trees. I wonder how we will hunt the seals; do they snare seals, like we did with rabbits in Good Hope?

My father finally relents, extracting promises from me regarding listening to my elders and making sure that I cover my face and wear my snow goggles. (The wooden carved ones that tie around my head with a caribou hide thong)

This is so exciting! Alice has two sisters and three brothers, her parents of course and an Aunt and Uncle accompany us on this trip. We divide people between sleds to equalize the load. Komatiks have wooden runners with cross support sections that are lashed together with caribou lacing. The size of them depends on the builder's wants and needs; average length is probably eight feet long.

Runners are often reinforced with some type of metal along the bottom. Snow or ice is melted and spit on the metal rails to help them glide fast through the snow and over the ice packs. Lead lines to the skidoo are 10 to 20 feet in length depending on how rough the sea ice is. A long lead line allows the skidoo to get over the ice and pull the weighted Komatik up and over behind it. There is no traction being balanced on the top of an ice pack.

Going out for even a weekend requires a lot of gear. The snow is too soft to make igloos so we will be spending the nights in canvas tents. On the Mackenzie River we used spruce trees as support poles to hold the walls of the tent up and keep it from becoming a kite. We also used spruce boughs woven together to cover the floor and keep us warm, there are no trees, how will this work? Speaking of kites, we will be using a kite to hide behind to hunt seals.

We start off at six in the morning while the snow is still hard, as the sun heats the snow it gets soft and makes it difficult for the skidoos to pull the weight of the full Komatik. Camp needs to be made by noon. It seems to me that we are heading out into empty white nothingness. How do they know where the seals are? There are no game trails, how do they know where to go?

Seals live under this massive expanse of ice, in front of us are miles of white, the edges of the world drop off with the curve of the earth and the blue sky reaches up to god. There is a small black line way off to the right on the far horizon. Sunshine and millions of snow diamonds glint back in radiant light. We are very, very little out here.

It is a strange feeling being the only visible creatures in this expanse of total white. The small black line is growing; it appears to be floating above the sea ice. Droning engines on the skidoos bring us closer to the line. We sit high on the Komatik perched on caribou hides for warmth with our mitted hands tucked under the ropes that tie the load down and keep us onboard. Sometimes the skidoo disappears from sight and sound and we swish through the sugar snow. Slowly up the ice packs we climb and then crash, the front of the sled slams down hard on the ice as we begin our decent down the backside.

Travelling by Komatik starts off as fun, but after a few hours we are growing tired of the continual bang of the sled. Look in the sky; what is it, look, look… holy what is that? The black line has become a floating Island with a mirrored image of land thrown high upwards into the heavens, an hourglass connection to the earth. The "Hallelujah" mountains in the movie Avatar may have been conceived from the visuals of mirages on the sea ice, but somehow I doubt it. There are no waterfalls and absolutely nothing green to be seen anywhere on this floating "mountain", to see islands floating in the sky is mostly unbelievable. The concept for the Hallelujah Mountains must have come from a Ocean in a much warmer place.

Camp is positioned just below the floating Islands on the ice; white tents on white snow with a wall of soaring black stone as a backdrop. The Islands fade as the sunlight changes. Our fifty-foot wall drops and becomes a twenty-foot bump on the forever ice. There is an expandable pole to hold up the centre of the tent and the sides are restrained by tying them to the Komatik. With the skidoos freed to go and hunt, we remain in camp to set up; I will have to wait to see how they sneak up on the seals.

In the spring the sea ice thins as the sun warms the solid frigid surface. Seals have air holes in the ice and as the sun melts the surface ice, the holes get bigger. Seals come up on the ice surface to bask in the sun laying beside their lifeline…the holes in the surface that are their escape routes back into the liquid ice of the Arctic Sea. Hunters hide behind a "kite" made of white material, usually a bed sheet and stealthily get close enough to the seal to get a head shot. If they hit the seal in the body, the seal will drop back into the hole and disappear into the sea. In order to have fresh food for the spring breakup, headshots are necessary.

Hunters return to camp with four seals. The seals are already rigid in the cold of the early evening; the heat of the sun runs quickly away into the dusk. Stiff seals are stuck into the snow and become anchors for the tent. Inside the tent we have laid down caribou hides with the hair on the ice, then we layer more hides on top with the hair facing up. Caribou hair is hollow; this provides insulation from the solid ice floor beneath us. For heat we have the primus (Coleman stove) with seven of us crammed into the small space it is still cool enough to see your breathe, but warm enough to take your atigi (parkie) off.

We are left to our own amusement, which turns into multiple games of cards and cats cradle. It seems that the adults have been brewing their own source of entertainment, raisins, sugar, yeast and maybe a potato is the usual bouquet of this drink in the north. It has been determined that in order to enjoy the juice of their labour it is better to leave town rather than risk having the brew pot stolen.

Laughing erupts from the tent beside us as night finally decides to brush a black wing over the skies. My friend's sister, a much younger girl possibly eight years old is with the adults. "How come Sally is drinking homebrew with them?" I ask. "She likes it," is the answer. What do you say to that? We return to the card game.

Morning arrives with the smell of boiling willow Ptarmigan. This is not a good thing. Heads peek out from under big five star sleeping bags. The bottom sheet on our bed is a raw tanned caribou hide, hair is everywhere. I drowsily lift my head, trying not to swallow the hair that has filled my mouth though the night. On the Coleman stove, which is in the centre of the tent, a big pot is filled with whole ptarmigan. (No feathers)

The pot has come to a rolling boil and the heads of the ptarmigan bob with the boil. Eyes bulging from tiny heads are in direct line of sight with mine, and only inches away. Open beaks appear to gasp, "save me, save me." Ptarmigan that have been eating willow buds for weeks smell powerfully acid and wild. This will be breakfast. I'm the new kid on the block; I like ptarmigan, but have never had them cooked quite like this.

No one has a problem with my ignorance; everyone is smiling big smiles and showing me the delicate method of poking out the grouse eyes as Hors d'oeuvres and biting the beak and sucking out the control panel. In deference to my hosts I suggest that they have my share of eyes and cranium. Chewing on the tough stringy bird with innards intact is as much as I can deal with on this maiden voyage.

For dinner the evening before, we have frozen raw Arctic Char and frozen raw Caribou, base line sushi. Condiment of salt, that's it, no wasabi. I found both to be good, I did not like the sensation of big chunks of slightly thawed Char so much and tried to swallow it quickly, this is fast food when there is no wood to build fires to cook your food. There is the MOST wonderful bannock and we fry Pilot Biscuits in canned butter and smothered them with strawberry jam, an Easter Feast!

P.S. Happy Easter everyone. It is way past the time for me to thank my Mom, Pat Kostelnik for providing me with pictures from the family collection. There is difficulty trying to find pictures of quality when they come from so far away and so long ago…thanks mom.

COPPERMINE

SCHOOLS OUT FOR SUMMER

In the back of a station wagon five kids pause in their bickering to push noses up against the long side window of the car. Dusk is creeping down the sharp mountain canyons casting a rosy glow over the limestone and shale. Far, far below on the curving highway along the Columbia River, a huge drive-in-movie screen is flashing pictures; we can hear cars honking as the previews for the movie begin to dart across the screen. Our most recent favourite song is playing on the radio, "in the year 2525 if man is still alive, if woman can survive..."

Our car speeds off into the night, we strain to catch the last glimpse of the drive in movie screen, Chitty, Chitty Bang Bang is the feature film tonight we read. "Can we go, please can we go?" We are travelling late this night, looking for a family friendly motel in our short detour off of the Crowsnest Highway on our way to Vancouver Island in B.C., Canada.

We had flown out of Coppermine a few weeks previous. Our trip began in Fort Smith, N.W.T. Dad has to take a course here before we can fly into Edmonton and continue our summer holidays. Angelina, my blood sister is flying from Fort Good Hope to meet us in Fort Smith and will continue south with us. This is her very first trip away from her home, the small village of Fort Good Hope population of 450 native people, located on the McKenzie River in the far north of Canada. I have not seen her since April when we moved from Good Hope to Coppermine, I can hardly wait.

Lorraine, a nurse that was stationed in Good Hope, married John the local R.C.M.P and they were transferred to Fort Smith. Lorraine is taking us on a tour of Wood Buffalo National Park. We are touring the park in Lorraine's baby blue love bug, a VW Beetle.

A cloud of dust approaches on the dirt road, Lorraine is a tough Aussie Sheila and she pushes the pedal to the metal, we will find out first hand what is causing the cloud. We are engulfed in the fine flour powder of dust, she hits the brakes, coughing we rush to close the windows that my little brothers are fascinated with! "Look, look when you turn these knobs the windows go up and down,' amazing, the windows are up, the windows are down, they don't remember much about cars.

As the dust clears, we find ourselves surrounded by behemoth brown bodies; they dwarf the car. Nasty pointed horns could pierce the little Bug and throw us in the air we figger. "Shh-h-h, quiet don't make them mad," a cow Buffalo brings a wild white ringed eyeball right up next to the window, "don't move, don't breathe," she snorts in disgust at the smell, as the human innards of this strange blue animal struggle to maintain silence inside of the flimsy "protective" shell.

Feisty Lorraine decides to push forward, slowly, she edges us out of the herd, we are clear, again the pedal is put to the metal and we decide that we should look for tamer challenges, like finding ice cream while we wait for Angel to show up on the plane.

My aunts live on ranches in Maple Creek Sask.: this is our most easterly point of venture. Horses, cows, chickens and pigs are all amazing. Rick and Rob our cousins teach us how to rope and ride pigs, Angelina is disgusted by the smell of the strange animals and she is NOT getting on the back of any horse, not a chance. She is having difficulty with the food. Fresh cows milk is something that none of us are used to and having it delivered warm from an udder to the table and having an appreciation for this "freshness" may need to be learned.

Hard-boiled eggs are good, but she peels off the white part. I think she may get sick from eating so much watermelon. In Edmonton 10 lbs. of bananas were on sale for 1$. The back seat of the car is still home to at least 20 lbs. of slightly bruised and brown bananas. Ice cream is heavenly; mom takes us for banana splits at Dairy Queen. We decide that a banana split is the perfect food. Chubby chicken at the A&W is Angela's and mine favourite, the boys order burgers. "Holy look, the girls are hanging our food on our car door, we can talk to them on that phone thing." We don't understand that we have to give the glass root beer mugs back.

Angel is pretty homesick after two weeks of ranch life and driving around in cars eating strange food. We are headed west and stop back at my Grandparents. My grandma, whom we called Nan, makes her special version of macaroni and cheese, Angela eats and eats like a starving person, Nan hugs her; a bond is formed. Angela seems to feel better after this and starts to try new food.

At Saratoga Beach on Vancouver Island we have rented a cabin for a week. My mom is from Comox and she hasn't seen her Island sister in years, we come to visit and swim in the sea. This ocean is much warmer than the Arctic one we live by. There are seashells, which we don't see in the Arctic Ocean, it smells really funny, kinda stinky we think, but we don't want to hurt mom's feelings, she looks so happy.

She shows us sea cookies (sand dollars) and whips and cracks kelp on the beach and tells us to jump on the bulb to make a loud pop. My uncle brings sacks of oysters down to the shore and we roast them on the beach fire we have built. We decide to leave these things with the green guts for the grownups.

Floating logs become our ships, our skin wrinkles from hours of swimming, noses are covered in freckles and sunburn, Angelina, with her browner skin burns faster than we do we find out. Now we have to swim in sloppy tee shirts to protect our peeling shoulders. There is no deadly sunscreen, people believe that the sun is good for you, how did that change?

At least in the ocean we don't have to keep taking showers before we can swim. Can you imagine, they make you take a shower at the swimming pool? We dont understand why they want us to get wet before we get wet. Kurtis was worried that they would make us take a shower when we crossed over the Alberta border into B.C. we are getting pretty tired of all of the rules.

In Banff National Park the boys weren't allowed to kill the gophers. They almost had them before Dad stepped in. An older lady looked like she was going to have a heart attack, I guess she didn't know that we could make a fire and eat them, maybe she wouldn't have minded so much then.

Something special is happening, we can feel it in the air. There is no one on the beach today except for a few kids. Mom and Dad keep hanging around the radio in the station wagon.

We don't bother getting a cabin with a T.V. We watched T.V. at our grandparents; we are only allowed to watch Bonanza and Ed Sullivan. If we want, we can watch Lawrence Welk as well, I've tried to watch it with my grandparents because it is their favourite show on T.V. It is very hard to sit that long for something that moves that slow. T.V. is just too boring; the ocean is alive with adventures.

"We now believe that anything is possible!" Mom and Dad are sitting in the front seat of the station wagon looking at each other in astonishment. Angelina and I climb in the back seat, we know better than to interrupt the adult conversation. We strain to hear the radio; it sounds pretty technical, but it is sure causing excitement amongst the grownups on the radio also. Across the airwaves we hear, "that's one small step for man, one giant leap for mankind." Neil Armstrong is walking on the moon; it is July 21, 1969.

P.S. Have a great summer everyone, the Captain and I are heading south to board the Audrey Eleanor in Pender Harbour. We will be taking her to her new berth in Powell River. I will be "off the air" with the White Girl Series until the fall. You know what Audrey's like; she's going to try to talk us into an Adventure. If she does we will keep you posted.

Happy Sailings to the Three Cheers, our good friends Siggy and Terrylynn Gold are on the move and we wish them the best in their summer travels. We expect to share an anchorage or three with them in the Broughtons in the fall. Cheers and safe harbours.

COPPERMINE

SETTLING INTO THE DARKNESS OF A POLAR WINTER

Our school continues to grade eight. Grade eight and grade seven share the same classroom. If we were still living in Fort Good Hope N.W.T. I would have to go to the hostel in Inuvik for grade seven. I now live in Coppermine, which is located on the shores of the Arctic Ocean in the North West Territories of Canada. It is also known as Kugluktuk and is today located in the newest Canadian Territory of Nunavut.

Grades seven and eight have one teacher, Mr. Adams. Mr. Adams is a legend amongst his students; he arrives at this stature in a short time. He is British and has a decisive and clipped accent; he comes to school in pressed shirts and demands our full attention at all times. If you do not pay attention or address your classmates and teacher with respect there are consequences. The dreaded "dictionary" was common punishment. There is also the opportunity to get the slipper, but it was a dire situation that dictated the boys bend over in the classroom and get their butts smacked with a running shoe. Girls had to hold out their hands and get the "slipper" across their palm.

Dawn Kostelnik with Grace Elgok and her little sister Patricia, Dawn has a baby on her back inside the itigi.

It was more a punishment of humiliation rather than corporal, the application of the slipper. The punishment of dictionary was torture, absolute and pure torture, give me the slipper! Gossiping in class may constitute having to copy two pages of dictionary, which is two pages but really four sides out of the Oxford Dictionary. We were made to copy the dictionary pages word for word; accents, hyphens all of those piddly squiggly things, part for part, and sometimes he checked it! Other times he would stand in front of the class and without a glance at the work, rip it in pieces. You never knew what he would do; the chance was not worth the possibility of having to do it over again in triplicate.

Jonah is in my class. His dad is Charlie Avakana Klengenberg, a famous carver of soapstone; he had some of his work on display in Montreal at Expo 1967. Jonah is an artist as well, he traces and draws out picture of the Roman Empire, we are studying the Roman Empire. Jonah grids out squares and re-constructs his pictures into huge posters that line the walls of our classroom. Mr. Adams takes a lot of time with him; we can all see that Jonah is gifted.

I love being in Mr. Adams class. He teaches us that there is an exciting world beyond the boundaries of sea ice and snow. It is cool to learn new things, I feel free to be curious without being condemned as "trying to be teachers pet", Mr. Adams wants to teach us about the world, he likes to teach. My classmates are interested in learning as well. Sometimes the questions get crazy, everyone talking at once, so excited about the new things Mr. Adams is saying, he laughs, not often but he knows he has stirred up all of these kids. It is such a beautiful big world that we live in.

"Quiet, quiet, back to work students!" Heads bend over books, we are curious to see what the books say about these crazy Romans. How their greed for power and "stuff" crashes their world. One hand goes up, then another, "Mr. Adams, why they're not happy to live in a warm place and eat them sweet dates growing on trees?" "They are warm, they can't freeze or run out of bullets, what's wrong with them peoples that they fights all the time?" "P-s-st anyone see fruit growin on trees, must be magic huh?" "Whas dates anyways?"

Lunch hour and recess we get access to the gym when it is colder than -30f. If it is warmer than -30f we eat lunch in our classrooms and are herded out side for exercise. Scrap pieces of cardboard are horded to be used as sleds. These are stashed under the school steps and get smaller and smaller as we abuse them sliding over rocks and gravel. At -30 and with access to the gym, we slam bodies and walls with volleyballs in extreme dodge ball. The ceiling of our gym is too low to play basketball or volleyball, we compromise, this is a spare classroom with wire mesh to protect the windows.

Bells ring and we return to classes. Often kids from other classrooms sit in the hallway reading comics and National Geographic's until they have learned to adjust their attitudes. If they had been old enough to read the words I suppose that reading the National Geographic's would have been an education in itself, they have great pictures. All the boys want to see the pictures of the half naked women in far away "south". Some kids spend most of the school year in the hallway "adjusting" their attitudes. In Mr. Adams class we learned, he did the adjusting cause he thought we were worth it.

An Inuit Elder arrives in the afternoon to teach us Inuktitut. We are learning both written and spoken language. Written Inuktitut has been adapted from the Cree syllabury in the 19th century by British missionaries. I do not have the keys to show you what the words look like. They are triangles and boxes with circles and accents, I find the written words easy to learn, I struggle with the language. Annunciation, seems to originate in the throat, I am not good at this. In my embarrassment at my accent I learn to read the words but my development in speaking the language is limited.

After school some of the older boys are allowed to use the gym to practice their music. We hang out side of the doors listening to the screech of an amplifier gone wild, twangings of an electric guitar that has escaped from its musician; we cover our ears and laugh. They are taking turns deciding who will be the singer. There is an electric guitar, a bass guitar and the drums, Philip plays the drums.

"I see-ee a ba-d-d Moooon" the voice breaks up and straggles off in the distance, we can't tell who is auditioning. A stronger voice picks up the tune " I see the Bad moon rising!" It sounds like Jonah. They try again and again. Now they are stomping their Kamik clad (leather home made shoes) feet to the beat of the song. Full on now, "I see the Bad moon rising, I feel trouble on the way," we accompany them out in the hallway. "Man those Eskimo boys can play Credence!"

We are without television and radio, but the doors to the outside world swing both ways. Flights to Yellowknife N.W.T. are a few times a week. The "sched" flights are a form of entertainment for the community;

families with children walk down to meet the plane and see who's coming in and who's gettin a parcel. "Ah-h-h, old Henry comes home from Camsell." (Charles Camsell Hospital in Edmonton) "My-y-y his kids is all grown up, he is sick with that T.B so-o-o many years." "His kids don know hes comin, get his kids, quick."

"Henry, Henry, its so-o-o good to see you!' everyone shakes hands and smiles, then shakes hands again and again. An old woman with tattoos etched on her face breaks through the crowd; it is Henry's sister. Tears stream down her face, she grabs her brother's hand, she has not seen him for 10 years, rubbing her nose on his she jerks his hand up and down in her excitement. "I was sure you was dead, I was sure you was dead." "Peoples what goes to the hospital comes back dead!" Drum dance tonight for sure!

P.S. This is a long time in coming Mr. Adams, wherever you are. The last I heard of your whereabouts through the moccasin telegraph, was that you were teaching in Fort Simpson, N.W.T. I would like to thank you for caring enough to ensure that we learned about the world and what we would need to participate in it as responsible adults. You taught me to love learning, I don't know how you can thank someone enough for that, but I do thank you.

COPPERMINE

THE NIGHT BEFORE CHRISTMAS

Twas the night before Christmas and all through the houses, not a creature was stirring not even the mouses. (Nee lemmings) All of the people of Coppermine were dressed in their finest with care, Itigi's (parkas) and Kamiks (home made skin and leather shoes) and clean underwear. Round-faced babies sing Jingle Bells with gaps in their teeth, Old James the Shaman snores in a warm corner, his dog tucked underneath. A roar of engines signals that Santa is near, this special delivery requires more than just reindeer.

The moon on the crest of hard packed snow illuminates his landing path so far below. Twin props swirl up snow crystals and with a roar and a rush, Santa's silver rocket quiets down to a hush. A side door pops open with a click of some gears and what to our wondering eyes should appear, but Santa the pilot and his co-pilot, Rudolph the Red- Nosed -Rein -Deer. "Hey Johnny K you and your crew, pull up the sleighs and rev that ski-doo. Get this crate unloaded for I have far to go, and I am seriously looking forward to heading south; WHERE THERE IS NO SNOW and they have never once experienced 40 below!

All year long the Community Hall rents reels of movies that are flown in once a week from Yellowknife, N.W.T. Volunteers set up the metal and wood chairs for the show on Wednesdays and again for the kids on Saturdays. We take turns selling drumsticks and ice cream sandwiches' for twenty-five cents each; admission to the movie is ten cents. The ten-cent admission means that everyone gets to go. This money is saved all year long and goes toward a special treat for the whole town.

My dad and several men are down on the sea ice as the plane arrives. They will pick up the surprise and bring it up to the Hall. The DC3 pilot tells my dad that he will "never do that again, how will I ever get that smell out of my plane??" "Merry Christmas, Merry Christmas, thank you very much!" Everyone shakes hands and wishes him well on his return trip back to Yellowknife and his family. "Merry Christmas and Happy New Year to you and your family!"

Doors to the hall burst open with a cloud of frozen condensation, everyone turns in anticipation, "Holy, can you believe what we are having for Christmas Dinner?" "We are having Kentucky Fired Chicken!!" "No, no it is Kentucky FRIED Chicken with eleven herbs and spices, it is made in Yellowknife!" Red and White coloured buckets of chicken and boxes of mandarin oranges make their way onto the long tables. There is enough KFC for everyone to have three pieces. There are 1200 people in the community hall; this means we have 3,600 pieces of chicken to distribute. Girl Guides quickly begin to hand out the chicken, the oranges are wrapped in thin green tissue paper, most everyone has never seen these orange orbs before. "Amah Amah, I can take the skin off by myself, look how easy!" "Oh My how good it is!" "Try it, try it!" "Should we eat this orange skin too?" "Yuck!"

We get two oranges each and a small bag of hard Christmas candy, swirls of colours melt away in mouths that smile with red and green teeth. Mrs. Priest hands out small packages for the kids, she is a Pentecostal missionary. People from her church in the south send up care packages for her missionary work. Sometimes they send up strange things like shiny black shoes with little straps, your feet would freeze off!

Most everyone has a full belly and sits back with a smile as they watch the slowpokes eating this chicken with eleven herbs and spices. Old James has no teeth; he needs someone to chew it for him. Mothers chew food for babies and pass it from mouth to baby bird mouth. Babies get tucked back into Itigies for a nap with full tummies too.

Old Annie wants to dance. Her face has deep groves around her mouth and eyes. Black Tattoos outline her eyes and define her high cheekbones. Silver and black hair stands wild up above the fur ruff of her Itigi. Her eyes flash a challenge as she picks up a drum. These drums are about three feet in circumference, she handles it easily. Her stick raps a rhythm on the edges of the wood rather than on the surface of the taunt dried skin that covers this circular instrument. With graceful twists of her wrists she begins to tap out a rhythm that follows the beat of her heart.

A group of spectators has formed around her. Everyone wants to watch her dance and sing her storey. She swoops with the drum; her song rises in a chant. Faster and faster she goes, eyes are widening in amazement, no one has every seen this dance that she is doing. All of a sudden she drops the drum. Her tiny bent body begins to gyrate in a dance that is causing even more wonderment. What is she doing? Her full fur trimmed Itigi swings and sways around her hips?

Her head comes up and a big smile reveals that she needs some teeth. Grinning from ear to ear she twists to Elvis playing a song in her mind. We all laugh, some little kids copy her and fall on the floor in glee. (It is Christmas after all) Our homegrown version off Credence Clearwater Revival starts to warm up guitar strings at the front of the hall. It only takes a minute and the dance floor is full, parkas are pulled over heads and thrown in a pile.

Wide eyed babies are pulled from their mothers backs and set in the pile of clothing that is growing, everyone watches for the babies, one of them could get lost in the mountain of cloth and fur. Kids dance with Grandmas, there are no particular partners, everyone just dances! Chairs are pushed back against the wall as the dance floor fills. This dance will go until the Coppermine CCR needs a break, then award winning fiddler Colin Adjun will cause feet to flash as no one can resist a jig or three. Coppermine Credence will come back once they've had their fill of jigging and Annie may pick up her drum again.

Christmas morning involves church. Catholics are a minority in Coppermine; most people are of Anglican or Pentecostal faith. I am glad to see that Mrs. Priest has lots of families in her church here, there weren't many that went to visit her and Mr. Priest in Fort Norman, it was mainly Catholic there. My family attends Mass with the Niptanatiaks, the Gaus and the Elgoks. After church the visiting starts. Everyone comes to our house for tea and cookies and cake. My mom spends a lot of time baking.

All day long people stop in to say hello and wish us a Merry Christmas. We play lots of cards here; we got a brand new game called Monopoly for Christmas. The Anglicans seem to think its OK to play cards. It is great to learn all of the new games! Double solitaire is my favourite, I wish I could remember how to play that game; it uses two decks of cards. We played cards on the Mackenzie River too, but we didn't talk about it much.

I get to pack the babies around so their moms can relax; there are a lot of babies. The babies ride on your back under your Itigi, a belt or rope is tied under their bums and around your waist so they don't fall out. Sometimes they pee on you. It is so much fun to have everyone visiting, shaking hands, some of the older people still rub noses. There are not many presents, lots of food and dancing, smiling people, how nice, I love Christmas!

P.S. We wish you a Merry Christmas; we wish you a Merry Christmas and a HAPPY New Year.

COPPERMINE

BITING THE HAND THAT FEEDS YOU

Running, laughing with his face buried in the fur trim of his parkie, a small boy succeeds in out distancing his friend who is also running as fast as his tiny legs will carry him. His friend is trying to catch him and take back the boys favourite stick.

The boys, one white, one Inuk are small for their age, they will both attend "beginners" a form of kindergarten in the coming fall, they are five years old. Both boys stumble over stones wearing their black and red gumboots that don't quite fit.

"Kurtis-s-s," wails his buddy, "give it back, give me my stick!" Kurtis knows he's winning the race, in his exuberance he forgets where he is. Little hands in mittens swing outward as he struggles to maintain his balance on rolling rocks in too big gumboots. Jaws of steel clamp on the edge of tiny fingers and the trap is set, death can be your shadow in the Arctic. The little boy is pulled into the dog line.

His small body is caught up and tossed and shook in the carnivorous

John Kostelnik and his team of long-legged, blue eyed 'Indian' dogs as described by Larry Adjun. The lead dog in this picture is Ace

clenches of a sled dogs steel jaws. On the wind swept rock a chorus of dog howls begins as soon as the child is captured. It quickly turns into a frenzy of cries for blood as the huge lead dog attempts to tear through the outer shell of the parkie and maul the tender innards cocooned within the stroud and canvas covering.

Like the body of a broken and dead rabbit, the child is thrown as if weightless by the strength of the jaws of the dog. Dogs leap frantically at the end of their chains, these are our pups, we raised these guys from babies, a primal urge stronger than they are captures them in the kill. Blood covers eyes in the ageless dance of the hunt and death.

"What's going on over at the dog line?' Joel and Simon look at each other, they laugh, that bag of rags that Ace the lead dog is throwing up in the air almost looks like Kurtis, but it can't be. Kurt knows not to go near the dog line. A thin wail fills the air as a throat clenched in terror finally regains its vocals. "mama-a-a, mama-a-a, the little buddy calls for his first line of defense as he watches this giant dog trying to rip his friends arms off. He has realized the situation and begins to scream at the top of his lungs, "Help, help Kurtie is getting chewed up, that Ace is chewing him!"

Joel pushes past Simon and yells at our mom, "Get the gun, get the gun, Ace is chewing up Kurt!" My mom comes running from the kitchen, she doesn't stop to question my brother; she reaches for the first gun she sees in the porch. Door flung open wide, she brings the gun to her shoulder and takes aim. It's hard to make out where Kurt starts and that god damned Ace ends.

She brings the gun down and thinks to check for bullets as she heads out the door, the gun is empty…where are the bullets, where in the HELL are the bullets! A box of shells sits on the windowsill, she grabs them and try's to load the gun, her hands shake in terror and desperation, in haste bullets hit and bounce off of the floor, she manages to shove one in the chamber. The bullet is jammed, they are the wrong shells. She grabs the barrel and runs for the door prepared to save her son by using the gun as a club.

We are screaming for help, dogs are barking, howling, Ace the lead dog growls deep in his throat, Kurtis is quiet, there is no noise."Help, help us someone!" My brothers Joel and John and I along with our friend Simon are screaming and yelling and running for the garage. If mom makes it to the dog line with the gun, the dog will probably kill her too.

We are running towards the shop as mom is running toward the dog line. Johnny turns and starts to run with Mom, the man door to the shop opens and a dark face peeks out. In a flash the door is closed and re-opened, Charlie runs from the shop with a huge wrench in his fist.

My mother has fallen with the gun in her hand, the barrel breaks away from the stock, she's having a hard time getting up, she is hurt. Charlie runs just out of reach of the dogs snarling at the end of their chains, we have all grabbed big rocks and any type of weapon that we can find, we run trying to catch up with Charlie, we will help save our baby brother.

Charlie swings the wrench with all of his might at Ace; the dog has a death grip on Kurt. Blows land with a loud thud on his hind end but do not seem to affect him; he has Kurtis by the back of his parkie and continues to shake him like a dead rabbit. Again the wrench is swung and again the dog ignores the heavy armed attack. My mom stands with the broken gun in her hands, tears stream down our faces, Kurtis isn't moving.

Charlie finally lands a blow to a fore leg and the dog drops Kurtis. My mom grabs his arm and pulls him quickly out of reach of the dog's jaws. She picks the little body up gently in her arms and we follow her toward the house. Dogs now whimper in the background, there is no movement or sound from Kurtis. Tears run down our faces, no one wants to ask the question... is he still alive? What is left of him, he is really only a baby.

"Mom, mom. " we hear a weak little voice, "Mom, I think I was dead." Hysterical laughter breaks out as we all reach out our hands to touch him. "Gentle, gentle," my mom says, "we have to get him inside and see how bad he's chewed."

His tiny body is laid on the couch, my mom lifts off his parkie with careful hands, his face is milk white and he shakes in shock. "Dawn go and get a blanket and a pillow." His little arms are pulled out of his parkie, in a perfect circumference like a thick purple band we see where the dogs jaws have clamped down and covered the whole of his arm. His back has nasty big red and black bruising bites. The wounds are deep into the tissue and muscle, knots of damaged flesh but nowhere is the skin broken. My mom bends arms and legs, feeling ribs, checking for breakage, miraculously he is intact, he will be very sore for weeks and affected forever, but he has survived. He is alive. My mom's finger might be broken from the fall with her finger in the gun trigger.

"How are you Kurtie?" We all ask, "I was dead for sure," he says, he's only five years old. "When he's chewing on me I pull my hands in my parkie and cover my head so he can't stick his teeth in my eyes." "He didn't even chew my hands, see!" He proudly displays his rough little nail bitten fingers for inspection, he is amazed that they are still there; we can see this, he is so happy to have all of his parts. We are so very happy that he is still alive.

Ace the lead dog we got from the R.M.C.P. is still alive as well. My dad takes him to the nursing station for an X-ray on his front leg. If the leg is broken he will be shot. The leg is not broken; he is bandaged up and taken back to the dog line to be chained up. Ace came to us as a full-grown dog, he had one eye that bulged dramatically from his head, this was milky white and he was blind in that eye. What Ace's life had been like previously, we did not know, it appears that damage had been done. How do you fix that?

My dad did not shot Ace for attacking Kurtis. If Ace had been lose and attacked anybody my dad would have killed him in an instant. No one was allowed near the dog run. In the real world when the rules are broken, you pay the consequences. You are ultimately responsible for your own life, even if you are only five years old and are totally distracted by your favourite stick.

P.S. I have a wariness of dogs after years of living with many of them and having experienced this attack on my little brother. I am a recovering realtor. In that life, contact with dogs on private properties was common. I refused to show a house if the dog was either in the house or able to reach me when I approached the house.

Your dogs job is to protect his home, when you are not there they will attempt to do that to one degree or another and if they sense fear they will attack. From me, they sense fear; I have seen too much, experienced too much. A realtor that I had worked with, whom I believe had show dogs informed me that "if I got to know more about dogs I would not be afraid of them." Exactly how do you respond to such ignorance?

COPPERMINE

SOLDIERS OF GOD

'LEFT, RIGHT, LEFT AND RIGHT...girls, girls keep your eyes to the front, don't look at your feet!' 'And once again, left, right, left, right and split.' " No, NO! " By now the scratchy old 45-vinyl record has run out of brass instruments and drums. Round and round the needle scratches out chalkboard screechie noises that are amplified through out the empty community hall There is nothing that benefits acoustics in this vast open space. We stand with hands covering our ears.

"Girls, we will be representing our community when the Governor General of Canada, Roland Michener and his lady come to visit." "We will do ourselves proud, we are the marching soldiers of god!" "Now once again from the top!" With her authoritative British accent, Mrs. Priest is Commander in Chief of god's army in our Inuk village. She is the Pentecostal Missionary that is taking charge of the Girl Guides in Coppermine N.W.T., in northern Canada.

Mrs. Grace Priest in traditional caribou itigi, with a flock of her Inuk lambs

In her British heart she thrills to the discipline of a marching band. Why on earth a Missionary in Canada's Arctic has such a vast collection of marching military band music is beyond anyone. But a collection of vinyl records she has indeed. A stack of old 45 vinyl records sits in the place of honour beside the portable record player. No one is allowed to touch any of these treasures. Should the needle on the arm get broken, getting a replacement needle may not happen for six months, and by then it would be too late. The Governor General would have come and gone!

She senses that she is losing our attention; we have been promenading for almost two hours. In full girl guide uniform we march, left, right, left…then right wheel, left wheel," Gracie, slope the colours!" My friend Grace has the prestigious position of flag bearer. We wheel right and encounter our sister marchers wheeling left; we are to pass through each other's marching line in cross section and with perfect precision. When done right we are impressive.

In an attempt to keep us focused, Mrs. Priest has put on a "livelier" version of the same brass and drums. In quick time we proceed, Margaret is approaching me from the left with the devil in her eye. She is to pass in front of me but instead grabs my arm and swings me in a quadrille. Let the square dance begin!

In exasperation Mrs. Priest watches her formation of blue, break into laughing girls doing an Inuk square dance to British marching drums. Our fearless leader softens from Commander in Chief to Mrs. Priest, the childless missionary who has a group of silly daughters whooping around the floor of the parade ground in front of her. It is months till the governor general shows up after all, she smiles at our antics.

Clapping her hands, "girls, my girls, this is enough for today." "Join hands, we will sing Oh Canada and say the Lords prayer before you leave for home." Voices rise to the roof as we honour our country singing in high girl voices, the prayer is more subdued. At the end we turn and shake hands with each other yelling in exuberance "Good NIGHT Girl Guides!"

It is dark on the way home, this time of the year it is always dark. My house is before Grace's, I watch from the door until I can no longer see her. Once she is out of my sight it is only minutes for her to reach her door. This winter we climb through a partial tunnel of hard packed snow into our house. I live down by the sea; the other girls live up the hill by the school. It blows something fierce off of the ocean. It takes only a tiny obstruction to build up a hard packed snow bank.

Sometimes when we are feeling the devil in us, we put rocks on the road at the start of the white outs (Arctic winter blizzards). The rocks create a barrier that "snowballs" and morphs into a much larger obstacle. In the morning huge drifts have built up and the tractor has to come out to dig the road out again.

It is a really, really bad thing to do this. With the big drifts on the road, the fuel truck and water delivery trucks can't get through. My dad has to get David to start up the D6 Cat and plow out the road so that the other trucks can get through. They keep on wondering why the drifts happen in these strange places??

We have dug out a bank of snow that is of our creation… there is a maze of forts in our back yard under this snow bank. The snow gets so hard that even with all of its weight the Bombardier sometimes doesn't leave tracks on the surface of the snow. It is much warmer inside of our forts than it is outside. Once we get one room dug out there isn't much else to do but expand. Room after room is dug out of the snow that cuts like butter with a knife. Muffled sounds are heard from outside, what's going on?

Grace's uncle Allen has a surprise for us. We crawl on our bellies out of our almost igloos. Our outside pants are made of untanned caribou hide; this slides easily on the snow. The Caribou pants are short in length coming to the top of our kamiks. Our mitts are caribou as well with store bought leather mitts as liners. My dad's pants are made of Polar Bear.

What does Allen have? He carries something squirming inside of his Anorak. Gentle, like he is picking up eggs he reaches inside and brings out his hand. "What is it, show us!"

With two cupped hands he displays a grey puffball of the softest fur. There is no definition, the puffball is round and looks like a pompom. Suddenly it moves a bit, tiny feet stick out of the pompom. A whimper, and the pompom topples side ways. Oh my, what is this thing?" Gentle, gentle you can each hold one!" I get to hold the first one, I can feel warmth coming through the so soft fur, I rub my nose on it. It smells like a baby critter, smells sort of like a puppy. I know this smell but can't place it.

One after another he gently pulls these babies out of his parka. With our mitts thrown on the ground, we stand marveling at these tiny creatures. They are all making little mewing whimpers. What are they, where are they from?

Allen hunts the giant Arctic Snowshoe Hares out on the tundra behind our house. While he is out hunting rabbits he hears strange noises. Sound carries well on the tundra and in the cold clear air. He follows his ears and finds a den in the vast and frozen tundra. These babies have crawled out of an entrance that is barely visible in the white drifts. Snow has blown in and covered most of the entrance to the den. It appears that the mother has not been here for days. He walks back ward and begins to circle the den. There are no tracks, the mother must be dead, there is no sign of her. She would never leave her babies by choice.

The creatures have instinctively sought refuge back in their frosty home. He reaches his hand into the den, cautiously. Mom may be inside and wounded, she will give him a good chew if she can. Slowly he reaches in; one, two, three whimpering babies are stashed in his parka, three pompoms of plush grey fur.

"What are they Allen?" "What will you do with them, can we have one?" "They are baby White Foxes." "They look pretty grey to us." " They get white as they get older. What do you feed them?" "Canned milk and seal oil, they are hungry all of the time, I think they are starved!" "You kids can help me feed them," like the pied piper he heads towards Graces house with a herd of kids in tow.

P.S. It is stories like this one that make me realize how parts of my childhood were astonishing. Some of the things that we all experienced as children are gone and will never be seen again. Take nothing for granted, protect our earth.

COPPERMINE

BATH TIME

Black round rock faces escape from months of imprisonment below the ice and snow. Heat radiates back from the smooth rock "mountain" that provides the backdrop for the tiny village of Coppermine which is located on the shores of the Arctic Ocean. Small hands escape from mittens and crowd together on the warm dry surface of the rock, giggles escape from childish lips. Into winter weary palms the heat from the black stone creeps.

The warmth carries with it memories of days without itigies (parkies), kamiks (shoes) and endless sunshine. We all look at each other and smile; our eyes are shining, its s-o-o good to feel the heat with our little hands. There is energy from the northern spring sun that I have felt nowhere else in the world. It invigorates and warms past the surface cover of lardy white skin, or the smooth pale ivory surface of the Inuk. Sun pours life back into limbs and lightens minds that had gone into dark winter hiding places.

Over night the solid cliffs and banks of packed snow melt and trickle toward the ocean. Streams begin to run with the tinkle of tiny bells through the rotten candle ice. An indent in any surface becomes a pond, and then a lake. We have a big indent behind our house; first we had the pond, now we have a lake in our back yard. The dog run is high enough up the slope that our dog team have mud up to their bellies but don't have to swim. They jump hard at the end of their chains wanting to escape and be wild.

Puppies appear from under houses and yip bravely and with enough force that they stagger on new legs. Such vicious little critters, we pick them up and inhale their baby smell; a quick belly rub and they follow us everywhere. "Go home you babies, get back, stay…stay." They don't listen.

Our house sits up above the ground on pillions. We have a honey bucket for a toilet, but all of the grey water from the bathtub, sink and washing machine empty onto the frozen dirt. When the bathtub is emptied it flows warm to the earth below.

Of course we have pups, everyone has pups, there are no vets so the dogs aren't fixed. Trying to secure a female dog in heat is often impossible. Our puppies have decided that they prefer to crawl under the house and have a nap in the warm bath water; it is nicer than the frozen ground by their house. Whimpers are coming from somewhere; we can hear them, where in the heck are they? "Here puppies, here puppies, " they sound frantic and cry for help. We want to help, but where are they?

"Under here, under here, come look!" "What's wrong with them dogs? " " Get out of there you guys, come on, we have grub for you." They are crying full out now. For goodness sakes what are they doing? On our bellies we crawl under the house and over to where they are lying. "What in the world is wrong?"

They howl with fear, their mother is howling for them and the whole dog line is joining in, what a noise, it's worse than feeding time. These are scared puppies you can hear it in their cries. We reach over and try to pull them, they are being hurt, we hurt them by pulling on them. "Such a thing, how crazy is this!" We don't want to hurt them so we stop pulling, we don't know what to do, we better go get Dad.

"What do you mean the puppies are stuck under the house!" "What have you kids done?" "We didn't do nothin, they are just stuck or something they won't come out!" "Oh for god sakes, let's go see." We are lots smaller than my dad; he can hardly fit under the house with all of the ice build up.

"I don't believe this, you kids run over to the shop and get a chisel and an axe and hammer." We deliver the tools in a jiffy, the dogs continue to howl and carry on, too much noise! One by one the pups emerge from under the house, muffled chopping accentuated with @#&*@ goddamned puppies, goddamned puppies, continues on under the house until all six pups emerge, smiling, jumping and licking faces.

Clink, clink, they mill around our legs and run over to their mom yipping and barking accompanied by the clink, clink sound. Clink, clink we know where they go. Slabs of ice are frozen to their sides. They had a little nap in the bath water that was drained from our house when it was still warm; as they slept the water-cooled and then froze them into the ice. Clink, Clink the sound stays for days, and yes they went back and did it again and again!

My dad is down under the house; he has been down there a lot lately, chopping out the puppies. For sure you know what happens next, my mom is in the bathtub and lets the bath water go in the tub, my dad is under the house under the bathtub drain lying on the frozen ground. @#&* GOD DAMN could be heard EVERY WHERE! We run over the snow banks howling with laughter, out of sight of course.

Rolling on the ground we can hardly stand the pain in our stomachs, there could be nothing funnier, then clink, clink over the hill comes the puppies, we can't stand it, tears stream down our faces we are laughing so hard, puppies jump and lick our faces as we roll on the snow. Clink, Clink.

In our backyard lake we float on the winters garbage. My brother Joel has found some pieces of pallet and scrap wood that are his raft, with a pole he is maneuvering around the yard lake. He tentatively maintains his balance. Water is four feet deep in some places and is the temperature of liquid ice. Soaking wet Kamiks (shoes) are heavy, they have absorbed so much ice water that the cold wins and feet are frozen cold. We only have one pair of kamiks, it takes days for them to dry, there is no choice but to put on gumboots.

Black rubber gumboots with brick coloured soles are so very cold, even if they are not wet. The teenagers are cool and roll down the tops of them. Hard cold rubber rubs against soft skin and leaves raw sores on the backs of legs. They hurt my feet, I have worn mukluks (kamiks, shoes) for years and the shape of the boot feels wrong. My legs and feet ache from the way they fight against the shape of my feet and the cold they attract.

Small black plastic bag Islands drift about in the deeper lakes and ponds caused by the spring thaw. Boys just need to do weird stuff, they poke holes in the "islands" and raw sewage spills to mix with the floating dog dung. These are the honey bucket bags that escaped the honey wagon over the winter. Ah-h-h the smell of spring in the Arctic, lying under the scent of raw sewage is the waft of diesel and gasoline, simply lovely.

Sea gulls have returned, the kids have a new game, "fishing for gulls." A piece of seal blubber is attached to a fishhook and thrown into the water. Gulls squawk and grab the bait, as they fly away with the hook, the kids begin to reel them in. Most of the gulls simply regurgitate the bait; one tough old bird is refusing to give up his treasure and gets hauled from his flight back to the shore.

Beady gull eyes are red in fury; the fishing line is taunt and the little kid is almost on eye level with this tough old scavenger. Who has caught whom? A bit of line is let out. Instead of fighting the line, the seagull walks forward, a little more line is let go, the seagull continues menacingly towards his captor, eyes blazing with beak slightly ajar (he still has the blubber with the fish hook in his gullet) this is his war stance, he will fight.

The kid drops the fishing rod and runs for cover, crying. Flapping his wings the gull opens both beak and gullet and drops the chunk of blubber with the fishhook intact on the pebble beach. Back in charge of his life and lunch he daintily picks around the hook and swallows the fat. Just another day in paradise.

P.S. if it is your dog, it is your dog poop…pick it up, it's really gross.

COPPERMINE

NEW YEARS GRIEF

Something is wrong. It feels like I have just crawled into bed and closed my eyes after a long night of babysitting, a loud scream is piercing my ears and my brain is commanding that I pry open my heavy, heavy eye lids. I am having the most amazing dream of flashing sunlight dancing off of calm blue water, I am back at Pauline and Andres Lacoue's fish camp at the Ramparts just south of Fort Good Hope, an eagle spirals down the cliffs and starts to scream and scream and scream…

Something is wrong, really, really wrong! The eagle's scream in my dream has turned into the sound of the siren that is located not very far away from my bedroom window. The siren is sounded when there is trouble in this northern community of Coppermine located in the North West Territories of Canada's arctic. Our tiny Inuit community sits on the pebbly shores of the Arctic Ocean. This siren is seldom heard in the dark of the night.

My window is frosted over and frozen; Jack Frost must like my window. He has repainted it many times, it is thick with his art- work; the sill is a lump of ice at least 3 inches thick. I cannot see into our back yard where the town garage is located, the community Co-op sits next to the garage, which is across the street, and our school is further yet up the hill. Our "backyard" continues on forever to the south, if you were to start walking, you might bump into Yellowknife after a long, long while. This is Polar Night time, we have no sun, we get to bask in dusk for a few hours and then return to the endless night.

H-m-m, "red sky in the morning, sailors takes warning" comes unbidden and sings a ditty in my mind. I can see a red glow in the sky to the southeast. This is funny; you have to have a sun to have a red sky in the morning don't you? Flickers of light begin to jump skyward, I hear a commotion in the hallway, and my dad is running for the door. Crashing sounds in the porch as he looks for his parkie and mitts. What is going on? The siren continues to sound as the red sky turns into a red ball through the ice on my window.

"Fire, Fire!" I see dark shadows against the red muted ball that I have now come to realize is the community's Co-op. This is where people go to sew fancy Itigies (parkas) and create and sell one of a kind masterpieces carved in soapstone. Original lithograph prints line the walls; Nar whale tusks reach spired heights of up to 9 feet and are prompted up in a corner. Smells of raw tanned furs fill the air. Raw tanned means the skins have been scraped clean and sometimes salt cured, but when heated with the warmth of body or inside furnace there is a definite lingering odour of the past owner.

Sealskin jackets are sleek and shiny; pillow covers of sealskin are sold here as well as circular table centrepieces made out of dried wolf faces. John Alukpik has big bright oil paintings on display. Kalvak (a famous Inuit artist) stamped tablecloths are a rainbow of colours. My favourite pieces of art at this time are the soapstone igloos. The tops of the igloos are carved and cut so that the top half of the dome is removable. Inside of the igloo are tiny carved people and household items that depict the lives of the people who live in them.

My favourite last year was the dolls. Each cloth doll is dressed in the finest miniature Itigi, with tiny fur mitts and beautiful little Kamiks, her smile and almond eyes are embroidered in silk thread. I am too grown up for dolls now.

Itigies (parkas) with huge ruffs of fur are as varied as the people who sew them. Ruffs are two or three layers of fur, which are stiffened to stand high above the face of wearer. Ruffs are trim and frame out your face in your Itigi. Cotton cloth covers the exterior of the Itigis and comes in every colour and pattern imaginable. The Co-op brings material in, in bulk so that it makes it more affordable to the individual craftspeople. I believe that the cost of buying materials was due upon the sale of the product. This allowed people to continue to create beautiful works of art all year round when the limited Tourism market was sitting in the sun elsewhere.

On display in the Co-op are old treasures as well, ancient seal oil lamps and carved ivory tipped harpoon spearheads. Copper fanned oil lamps and tea pails, skulls of Polar Bears and tiny foxes. A Polar Bear hide that is tanned and mounted on red felt, it is so big that the front paws are secured to the ceiling and a hind foot drapes on the floor, this could all be lost in a flash of fire. Old whale bones that have not been used for carving lay under display tables. Porous bone from the whales creates a dynamic effect when figures are carved into this brittle, golden honeycomb that once carried life essential nutrients to its owner.

I've thrown my itigi and kamiks on, my mother and I are standing on the hard packed snow that has blown and drifted onto our front step, yet again. It is cold so very, very cold. I turn my head into my itigi it is hard to breathe; it hurts your lungs to breathe through your mouth. My left ear has frozen many times due to this bad habit. Noses frost up quickly as air turns into ice when it hits the moisture inside of your nostrils and condensates. A few streetlights that are in this area can only be distinguished by a faint yellow glow in the ice fog.

Flames are still dancing inside of the co-op; we can see them behind the glass window that faces our house. Shadows of people dart around the building, smoke swirls and mixes with the ice fog, people are in chaos after a night of celebrating the incoming New Year. Ladders are set up against the wall that is furthest away from the window, which is casting dancing hell lights on the snow. Skies have lightened as much as they will, we have a grey dawn. Ladders set up by one person are being taken and used by another; the only escape from the roof for some is to jump.

Hoses and water pumps are close at hand in the community garage, 300 feet is all they have to travel, they freeze. It is at least -50f. In the silver- grey morning, smoke from diesel-fired stoves escapes from chimneys and falls back toward the frozen ground. Sounds carry clearly on the cold air. "Watch out, it looks like it might go!" "No, we got to save the carvings!" Smells of burnt fur fill the air. Glass shatters and explodes outward from the building. I can hear my dad yelling "let it go, let it go!" "Everyone off the roof, she's going to go!" "Run, get clear, get clear!"

With a whoosh, a back draft of wind is sucked into the broken windows and the flames shoot skyward! I can hear my mom whispering, "oh no it is all gone, it can never be replaced!" A great quiet settles over the crowd. Black figures with slumping shoulders and drooping heads stand in silence or quietly kick at the snow with frozen kamiks. Crackling of burning wood and the drip and sizzle of melted snow and ice dropping into the inferno are all of the sounds we can hear. It is eerily quiet; someone has thought to shut the screaming siren off…finally!

All winter the burnt black and grey bones of the co-op stick through the snow banks and are all that remains of the heart of this Inuit community. In the springtime the town kids sift through the ash searching for treasure. We find coins from the till melted onto one another. Burnt soapstone carvings are black and the heat has cracked the bigger ones. My brothers pick up small-blackened lumps that have been passed over. It takes hours, but the boys rub and sand away the black and underneath gleams round-bellied Polar Bears (Nanook) and smooth, cool seals caught forever swimming in the green and grey of soapstone. From the ashes, new life begins.

P.S. Happy New Years Everyone, I believe that this new year of 2013 will bring peace and happiness to anyone who wants it.

COPPERMINE

HIGH FASHION

Grab her, quick, grab her, she runs fast!" I twist and turn; the fur rips on my long parkie. "NO!" I break away and run for an opening in the crowd, I sprint for the narrow escape route, someone knows my tactics, a leg is stretched out and I am tripped. With a hard whoosh the air is knocked out of my lungs as I hit the road; I feel like a giant fist has slammed into my gut. I lay on the frozen ground gasping like a glaze-eyed fish out of water, can't catch my breath, can't breath, but worse... they have me!

They whoop and holler in victory. "Come on Kabloonah, (white eyes) its your time, we have you now, might as well give up little girl, we GOT you!' "You can't get away from us, we have you good, say yer' prayers!" "ARE YOU READY?" I twist and turn trying to escape my captors. I have pulled my arms out of the sleeves and into my parka, this is worse; I am now in a strait jacket of my own device! (Funny how that happens) ONE, TWO, THREE, FOUR, with every count I am slammed to the ground.

I am reminiscent of a blanket at a blanket toss, hands have secured me at every possible inch, they take no chance that I will squirm away. My kneecaps and elbows feel like they are broken. My back and butt have lost feeling thank god, TWELVE, THIRTEEN AND ONE MORE FOR GOOD LUCK! Is it almost over, please let it be over! No, now we have the 'pinch to grow an inch' routine. Bee bites begin; my arms and legs are exposed to harsh and deep pinches that are Bee bites, not stings. Oh Joy and Happy Birthday to me! I lay in pain on the road long after they leave.

After school I had tried to deek out the emergency exit and make the break for home, no such luck, they spot me. Some ratfink ratted me out. In Coppermine this is the glorious tradition of Birthday Bumps! Some damned white man initiated the Inuit to this part of their culture and they expanded upon it! No one wants to acknowledge their birthday because of the trauma. I hope this "tradition" got lost along the way; some old ways are much better let go. This is not part of a birthday celebration that I remember with pleasure, I hurt for days.

This year for my birthday I dream of a new parkie. My old parkie is very long in length; way down past my knees this keeps my legs warm. It has no zipper. Zippers let the wind in, so no zippers for practical purposes. It is a solid green colour, one of the colours that the co-op has plenty of. There are lots of green parkies running around town. I have a basic ruff of wolf fur around my hood to protect my face. When you pull your parkie off over your head, the static electricity causes your hair to stand straight up and then stick to your face, there is no such thing as fashion. My green parkie is a little kid parkie or an old woman parkie; it is not a groovy young woman parkie.

Girls coming back from the hostels in the big cities of Yellowknife and Inuvik arrive in high fashion and style! They wear jeans and roll their gumboots down. Their parkies are short and have zippers. Very groovy girls! Our pants are stretchy and are weird colours. We get whatever the HBC (Hudson Bay Co.) has to offer or we can get sent up from the Woodward's catalogue, Simpson Sears doesn't ship to the north yet.

My mother orders what she likes, I look a little strange sometimes. I learn that clothes are only meant to cover our bodies and keep out the cold and wet. Hopefully I don't wear out what few things I possess until springtime, this is when the next clothes order is sent out. Mrs. Priest the missionary has taught me how to sew on patches though.

But oh my, I would love a nice parkie, a grown up parkie, I am thirteen years old now, almost grown up, I would love a parkie with a zipper and nice trim, any colour but green would be good! My fur on my very green parkie is wolf; it stinks pretty bad when it gets wet. I can only imagine having wolverine fur around my hood. (It doesn't freeze and stick to your face either) I should not expect a new parkie, my green one still has lots of life in it, there is no reason for a new one. I cannot imagine getting a new parka just because I don't like my old one; we have to wear old clothes out or out grow them in order to get anything new. Everyone is like that.

My dad must have heard my thoughts and wishes! He comes home with a surprise for me for my birthday. My Dad travels a lot in his work, he checks in on communities to make sure things are running smoothly, he has just returned from Cam Bay, Cambridge Bay, N.W.T. "I have something for you", he says. He is excited about his present. It is very big in the clean honey bucket bag. I can't figure out what could be so big that would be for me?

It doesn't take much to open the bag (there is no wrapping paper to be bought anywhere, and he is a dad) inside is something white and heavy. I pull it out of the bag, it weighs a ton, it is huge, a big white blanket?? There is not much definition to it. Oh, OK, I see a hood and arms; it is some type of parkie, very different. It is from the Eastern Arctic, they have a different style of parka in the east, the hood is very big, with a funny point at the top. There is no zipper and it comes down longer in the back than the front, but the front reaches to my knees, it is huge, I will have to tie a rope around the waist to make it fit. Every part of it is white, very white. How do I keep this clean?

He has a big smile on his face, "do you like it?" he asks with happiness in his voice. "Oh Daddy I love it!" What can I say? He is so very happy, I wanted something that wasn't green, I now have a parkie that is defiantly not green and for sure, not groovy. He is excited that it will keep me warm when we go sealing in the spring on the sea ice, "you can sneak right up on a seal with that on, you will have to be careful not to get lost in the snow, we will never find you." "No zipper so you can pull it right over your head and the wind won't blow through!" A perfect father parka!

My mother is looking at him strangely. "Johnny, did you forget the other present?" she asks. He looks back confused, "I am not sure, what other present?" "The one we talked about just before you left?" More bewilderment, my mother reaches behind her and pulls out another package. "This is for you Dawn." This is not usual in my life, two birthday presents does not happen. I don't know what to do, "thank you." I open the brown paper package and Oh my god!" Another parkie! Do I have to choose between the two? How could I not choose the parkie that makes my dad so happy?

This parkie is navy blue with a zipper and contrasting trim along the bottom, Wolverine fur around the hood and cuffs and bottom. IT IS BEAUTIFUL! I pull it out slowly, it is short, I try it on. It fits just right, just above my knees; I can run like the wind in this parka. "Do I get to keep it?" "Of course you do, you can have both." The Navy Blue parka is absolutely perfect, if I had sewn it myself I would have picked everything exactly like this, it is not at all practical, it is beautiful. I cannot wear this out hunting. My dad is not saying much, I guess he remembered hearing about a parka and small parts of the conversation, now I have two parkas, this in unheard of.

You only have one body; you can only wear one at a time, why would you have two? I know why I need two. "Dad, I cannot go out on the ice hunting with my groovy parkie, but I can go if I put my beautiful white parkie over top." "It is big enough to wear over top, I will be double warm, warmer than anyone, this is perfect, thank you so much." "In town I will wear my beautiful navy parkie to school, I have everything, I will be cool and warm at the same time, it can get no better!"

P.S. YAHOO IT IS RENDEZVOUS! Remember…there is no sweat in the ARCTIC, but tap er' cool, tap er' light.

COPPERMINE

NANURLUK, SUPER BEAR

Pierre Elliott Trudea is the Prime Minister of Canada. He will be doing a tour of the Arctic. The buzz around here is that he may be coming to Coppermine N.W.T., for a visit. Nothing has been confirmed, everyone is in a tizzy, we must do something special for the Prime Minister of Canada. What do you think that people from the "Outside" want to see when they travel to the Eastern Arctic? Why Polar Bears of course. They are known as Nanook in this area, that is what they are called in the language of the Inuit.

We have no Polar Bears, at least not on a regular basis like Churchill, Manitoba. They can conjure up the big Spirit Bears on demand there. How can anyone compete with that? Truth be told, we are really happy not to have the giant white bears hanging around waiting to eat us, or the dogs. I can't imagine bumping into one in a white out; it would be a big bump with bad consequences. Biting dogs are enough to deal with.

A few years ago a hunter travelled out on the sea ice to hunt seals. His family waited for him to come home, a storm blew in and he is late. Being a few days late after a storm is usual…he is still not home after a week. It is time. His friends and his son gather and form a search party to look for him, he has been out on the sea ice alone, far too long. They travel for two days, the hunting is not good this year, the hunter has to go far-r-r away to look for seals. "Nothing, nothing," he goes way-y- y out der'. A little black dot on the frozen white ocean is all he is.

"Look, look!" An arm points out direction jerking back and forth in excitement, "there!" An over loaded Komatik grows large in size as they approach, the skidoo is still attached to the sled. "Peter T, Peter T, where are you?" There is no answer in the still and empty space, not even an echo…there is nothing for a voice to bounce off of. Voices carry on and escape over the ice and snow and drop down into Russia to visit.

Two skidoos with three men have travelled long to find their friend and father. Both skidoos sit beside the heavy Komatik. Wind has drifted snow up against the sled rails and along the sides of the deserted skidoo, they have not moved for a long time. There are no tracks in the snow. Days back the frozen brush of wind and weather erased any tracks of man. It is getting dark; they need to make camp before night drops hard on top of them with its solid heavy black.

Something is dreadfully wrong. The rescuers set up their camp away from the Komatik; ghosts are pulling at their mitts and whispering in their ears. No one can say Peter T's name, no one is sure that he will ever come if they call him, they are afraid that his spirit will return and be angry with them, trying to call him back from the underworld. This is bad, very bad; they want to go home, they cannot return until they find him. Spirits are lurking, the men shut their eyes and try to shut out the ghosts! All night the spirits drift through their tent and breathe frost in their faces.

"He is gone to the sea, below the ice with the sea goddess Sedna" "But where?" "There is no break in the ice?" "We will make a circle for a mile and come back." "If he is still not to be found we leave, I won't spend one more minute with these demons floating around us!" No Peter T to be found. No one wants to open his Komatik, the sun warms up the dark tarped in load, a shift occurs, a huge hairy paw escapes the confines and drops to the ice floor, black skin, white fur.

"David, look, look, Nanook!" Approaching the sled cautiously, they untie the tarp. A huge Polar Bear is bundled up on the Komatik. A clean shot to the head had stopped this giant in his tracks; he must be eight feet long and weigh over 1,400 pounds. He is Nanurluk, Super Bear. Where is the hunter of the Bear? There is no sign of a struggle between the two. It was a death shot and only one shell that dropped him, where did Peter T go? Their skin crawls with the supernatural, the bear's spirit must have come back and swallowed him whole…and alive!

There is lots of gas in the skidoo and in the warmth of the spring sun it starts readily. David, Peter T's son is to follow his fathers Komatik; the other men take the lead with the Komatik in the middle. It takes several attempts to dislodge the big sled; it has frozen into the snow and ice of the Arctic Ocean. With a hard jerk the Komatik is free and everyone runs to jump on waiting skidoos.

"Ataataga, Ataataga "(father), sobs David. As the Komatik pulls ahead David sees a black bundle sunken in the snow. The men rush back to inspect the situation. Peter T is rolled over on himself and frozen stiff. Peter T has been frozen for a long time; they cannot straighten him out to load him on the sled with the Polar Bear. In the end he is tied on top of the bear curled up like a large baby, it is hard to secure him.

A somber team returns slowly to the village. It is a long slow trip home. There is not enough rope to keep both the bear and Peter onboard. Peter keeps slipping off. The horror of his death builds in their minds. Bear spirits rage and new demons are born and created in their imaginations as they slowly grind their way back home.

Peter T fell off of his skidoo. The Komatik with the weight of the great bear continued in momentum and rolled forward to capture and contain Peter T. He is literally rolled into a ball under the sled and froze to death. In his death the great white spirit bear quietly and thoroughly carried out his revenge on the Inuk man. Such power of spirit is legendary. No one will hunt Nanook for years. No Polar Bear killing will occur until this story fades out, or death by mauling is unavoidable.

We have a story of a Polar Bear to offer to Prime Minister Trudeau, we can guarantee no Nanook however. ' What else they crazy about, them peoples from the outside?' 'Ah-h-h they loves' igloos!' 'We laugh, we tells em' we live in igloos!' 'They believes it, them white eyes, is good, we make em' happy!' In school we receive letters from other schools south of our Canadian borders. Part of our curriculum is to return correspondence with assigned pen pals. We regale them with tales of eating raw bloody meat, which we do and living life in an igloo, which we don't. Most kids have never lived in an igloo even in the late 60's. So possibly we contributed to the lack of knowledge that our southern neighbours confirm in conversation when discussing Canada.

An igloo is built for the Prime Minister. Unfortunately he is not able to make the trip, the kids enjoy the igloo. In the spring the Honorable

Governor General of Canada Roland Michener will visit in his stead. They keep talking about securing sovereignty in the Arctic, I don't know what they mean but it makes me nervous.

The U.S. has DEW (distant early warning) line sites all across Canada's north. I stand beside my father on the shores of the great crystal waters of the Arctic Sea. Beside us is a man from the south who has come to test our water and our land, our home, our True North Strong and Free. He laughs; he has a meter that tells him how much radiation is in the water, he says, "gee, by the count on my Geiger counter you guys should glow in the dark!" This is how much radiation there is in the water and on the land and in the Caribou (Tuktu) in 1970.

P.S. In 1970 Prime Minister Trudeau travels to the Arctic with a stop in Yellowknife to officiate at the very first Arctic Winter Games. The 2014 Arctic Winter Games will be held in Fairbanks Alaska.

COPPERMINE

BLOOD LUST

THIS IS A DEVIATION FROM THE "FLOW" OF THE WHITE GIRL SERIES. WOLVES HAVE BEEN IN THE FOREGROUND OF THE NEWS AND I AM NOW PROVIDING ANOTHER FACET TO THE DEBATE.

Driven snow lashes bodies. Ripping and tearing the fingers of the furies grab at the hollow insulating hair on the backs of thousands of gods' creatures. Howling winds send stinging particles of ice that sandblast and freeze human skin on contact and hurl frozen glass like shards through the air. This cutting ice blinds big brown eyes and coats long eyelashes that are not human.

Ancient genetics become confused in the swirl of snow and white. A pathway too old to remember the beginnings of; is lost in a wave of snow. A sage leader with downcast head attempts to catch a glimpse or the scent of his trail, he turns back on himself, the herd follows and they begin to circle. Tighter and tighter, thousands upon thousands of caribou begin to build a vortex. They have struggled to find food for days and now they stumble and fall in weakness, they are lost in a high arctic whiteout.

Word passes as quickly as a thought through the small community, moccasin telegraph. Tuktu (caribou) are nearby. Hunters with ancient blood coursing through their veins are on alert. A herd this close to the village is not usual, excitement builds. Skidoos are fuelled and rifles loaded. In days of old, dogs were harnessed and spears sharpened. A good hunter might have spare spears or harpoons and arrows, but not as many as bullets. A spear could equate to a single kill, dogs don't travel as quickly as a skidoo can. The balance has shifted.

Two hunters per skidoo, one drives, one has his sealskin clad feet hooked through the bars on the side, he stands with his rifle ready, eyes straining for a glimpse of the herd. Exhaustion has slowed the milling caribou to a stand still. Engines noise and the smell of human is carried on the wind, this causes confusion and the herd trembles with fear. Escape, escape, danger comes, man approaches.

Bang, a nervous young hunter fingered the trigger. Like a start gun at a horse race this sets the herd in motion. Around and around they go, presenting a broadside target for bullets. They are as big as huge oversized birds in a shooting gallery and are totally vulnerable. Bodies fall and panic builds as individuals try not to tread on hurt family members. Thrashing hooves add chaos as the herd begins to break rank and flee for their lives. All order has become discord.

Bodies fall and blood covers the eyes of the hunters. Shot after shot is fired into the herd, animals are piling up on each other like badly stacked wood. Wounded caribou struggle to escape. Bloodlust covers men's hearts and fills the minds of the human hunters. Like a bad drug, killing flows in their veins. Shot after shot, animal after animal falls and dies or struggles to escape the killers.

As the skidoos rage around the perimeter of the herd the man standing on the back of the skidoo empties his rifle chamber and reloads yet again. People at their worst, like land sharks the smell of blood drives them into a feeding frenzy. They have lost all sense and all compassion; they have become something else, some other red-eyed animal. They now kill for the lust of killing. Yes, it is a lust, a bloodlust, humankind's shame.

Legs stick skyward through the snowdrifts; a frozen eye stares off into the dusk. Quiet covers the land. A huge weight descends with the quiet to blanket the hunters as they stand and stare at what they have done. Not a word is spoken. Realization of the pillage begins to pierce minds that are now numb with their wrongdoing. How could they have done this disgrace, how could they dishonour themselves and so many of their brothers? How can they live with their waste? White horn of splendid antlers rises to the sky in homage to the sacrifice given. The loss of life ranges in estimates of 4,000 to 6,000 animals. This wasn't the first and it wasn't the only massacre, I can only hope that as of today it would be the last.

This is a documented case of slaughter. Where it happened is not relevant anymore. It was an era of transition; what is the excuse for slaughter today? In times past, if there was no meat you starved. Animals were killed to allow humans to live. Dogs and spears have given way to skidoos and guns which give people the advantage. Traditional hunting grounds and herds cannot escape intact when faced with the bloodlust of men and non-traditional weapons. Mindsets of ancient times have not adjusted to the ease of hunting with machines. People need to realize that they do not have to kill every living creature in order to make it through the winter. Regardless, as little children we were taught to never waste a life.

I have seen this carnage and waste on the Dempster Highway on the Yukon side only a few years ago. Caribou were left dead within feet of the highway. Why do you kill for the sake of killing? If you kill the animal, honour it by using the meat to feed yourself and your family. If you kill it, you must eat it. Why else would you take the life of your brother?

Two major slaughters of this type are documented; other butcheries are miserable secrets that eat away at the people who participated in them. These are stories that need to be told so the disgrace is never repeated. Our children have to be taught to respect that the animals have given their lives to feed us. You only kill to eat and you are thankful.

"Long time ago this happened; them white men start to count caribou." They had troubles finding some and some had troubles counting the ones they found. After the great slaughter the white men could not find all of those caribou. Where do they go? They had big meetings about this, them Kabloonak (white eyes) where are the caribou? Did someone count too many sometime, is someone lazy and lie? No, no the figures all say the same; there are thousands of caribou missing. The white men visit the elders; do you know where the caribou went? "Haven't seen caribou for lo-o-o-ng time," the elders say."

This is true; the white men don't discover that the caribou are missing for a few years. There is a huge hole in this caribou herd that has to be accounted for. Who or what could kill that many caribou? Blame must be laid.

A wolf kill program is implemented.

Black and white opinions made life easier for me when I was younger. As I get older grey areas show up to present more options and cause confusion. It is easier to live in the "now." Deal in the present with justifiable righteousness, with only one probable option visible at a time, why bother to look for other factors, that only affect other times and other lives.

In the 1970's a group of "hippies" in Whitehorse protested the Alaska pipeline. My partner Rick Cousins moved to the Yukon in 1974 with hopes of working on this pipeline, I was protesting this pipeline with all of the vigour of youth during the day and holding hands with a pipeline welder at night. It's a good thing that at the time conversation wasn't our strong suit.

Our focus was so directed on preventing one particular pipeline that we forgot about the consequences as a whole. The pipeline still has not gone through. In our innocence, we actually believed that the U.S. had listened to us and had stopped its invasion. We were mighty; we had saved the caribou and land from great scarring. When they want something… they will come.

The reality is that they (U.S.) simply did not need it at the time. You know the rest of the storey, they ship the fuel on the mighty and non-containable seas and we murder the oceans. We eat what lives and grows in those waters Exxon Valdez and the Gulf of Mexico are well-documented oil spill "slaughters". If the fuel doesn't go one way it will present itself another. In these years of "wisdom", I would prefer to see the fuel transported through a pipeline on the ground; at least it would be semi-contained. I am forced to look at the many facets (the grey areas) that now present themselves.

Until we find an alternative means to fuel our lives, like a creeping tide of water the force of the fuel will find another way to market.

When holes are found in Caribou herds the animals without voices may not be the only ones that have contributed to the loss of life. Sometimes it is easier to place the guilt on beings that can't talk back.

P.S. The Population Status of Caribou in the NWT, by George W. Calef, NWT Wildlife Service 1979 is one of many sources that discuss caribou herd slaughters. This storey is told deep in the night, tears streaming down faces, the brew pot is empty. This is a deep hurt, a deep shame.

COPPERMINE

LAND OF THE RINGED SEAL

Sunshine glistens off of sugar snow, billions of tiny crystals sparkle like diamonds. Skies are deep, deep into blue. Squinting one eye, it is hard to gaze out over the frozen Ocean and not be blinded. Giving up in disgust, I pull my wooden ilgaak 'sun goggles' back over my eyes. While they eliminate the glare, I hate having anything restrictive on my face. My hood on my huge Eastern Parkie is thrown back; I want to feel the warmth of the sun full on, the winter has been long.

We are 30 miles out on the frozen Arctic Ocean; it is spring in the high Arctic. Spring means sunshine and rotten ice, not flowers and grass. It is the weekend before Easter and my family has escaped our house, which feels like it is shrinking in size daily. We have gone sealing in this vast and endless vista that is home to the Ringed Seal. A few families have ventured out this first, warm enough weekend of the year. It gets to -30F at night but warms up to -15F during the day.

My brother Joel is determined to shoot a seal. He is now 11 years old and feels that it is way past time for him to achieve this goal of manhood, bringing home food for his family. Tuktu (caribou) has been our mainstay for dinner all winter long, while I am not fond of seal, any change would be a good one. Cooked seal reminds me of cooked congealed blood. Seal liver is not to be eaten; the fat on seals has a very low melting point. When you clean them, the blubber melts on your hands. Fresh food is ALWAYS welcome.

My parents, my three brothers and myself are alone on this adventure. We leave our camp late in the morning. David and his family stay back to relax, they will head out on their hunt after we leave. They are an Eskimo family from the village of Coppermine where we all live. Our Komatik is loaded with survival gear and kids, we are going sealing!

My dad brought along two poles that are each four feet long. We have an old white bed sheet that will get tied to the poles, which are lashed together to form a cross. The effect of the effort is a large white "kite". This kite is used as a shield that you hide behind in order to sneak up on the seals. You need to be close enough to get a head shot.

With the beautiful warm weather and sunshine bouncing off of the snow and ice the surface of the frozen sea warms up and gets quite balmy. Seals are also tired of their home under the ice; they crawl up on the surface and bask in the sunshine. They have breathing holes hidden under snow; in the spring the holes get large enough for them to crawl through and this allows them to live topside for a bit. Ever weary, even the light and delicate music of tinkling ice may cause them to slide back to the dark depths of the liquid ice they live in.

Baby seals having no experience, will crawl up on the ice to bask in the sun for as long as they can. Warmth on the surface is deceptive and as they laze in the sun, their escape routes nee breathing holes freeze over. What to do? It must take them to the point of starvation before they begin trekking across the vast froze ocean surface. They are completely vulnerable, unless they can find another breathing hole that is open; there is no escape for them. The chances of getting out alive are next to nil.

Tracks of lost seals can be seen for miles. We have passed several of these trails today, none of them fresh. Our hunting trip has turned into a scenic tour, with no sightings of seals and no one really caring. The joy of being outside in the sunshine causes spirits to soar. Islands float in the sky, mirages caused from the heat of the sun on the frozen surface. The drone of the skidoo and swishing of the Komatik through the sugar snow is mesmerizing; it is good to be alive!

We are slowing down; my dad has stopped the skidoo, what's up? A fresh trail in the snow, we are close to a baby seal that has lost its way. "O.K. Joel, get your gun, we will go after this one." They re-assemble the kite and head down the seal path, holding their kite in front of them. There probably is no reason for this exercise, but this is a training exercise after all. Sneaking up on seals takes practice and is very difficult. There is no cover out here, no bushes to hide behind and sound carries long distances over the ice.

A seal must be shot in the head, it has to be an instant death or it will slide down the breathing hole and disappear into the sea. All in all, acquiring supper can be difficult. This baby seal has almost no possibility of cheating death. Wandering around the sea ice trying to find another open breathing hole is unbelievable odds. If he does not become our supper, he will most likely die slowly of starvation or become dinner for an Arctic Fox or Polar Bear.

It is a strange phenomenon, one minute we can see dad and Joel on this large flat surface, the next second they are gone. We listen, no gunshots can we hear, maybe that seal is making better time than we thought. He has to crawl on his belly on snow and over ice, how fast is he ? Poof, Dad is visible again. He waves to my mother to drive the skidoo over. Strange, we didn't hear a shot. Maybe the baby seal is already dead?

Joel has a huge grin on his face. Gee whiz, we missed his first hunt, too bad. He is bouncing on his feet he is so excited. "Look, look at this crazy thing!" Lying in the snow, beautiful glistening brown eyes limpid with tears and hissing with teeth barred is the 'helpless' baby seal. All eyes turn to my dad, what will we do? My Dad is pulling the bed sheet off of the kite.

Dad circles the baby seal with the bed sheet. Against all odds this baby is still not going down without a fight! We have never seen a seal killed this way, why doesn't he just get Joel to shot it fast? Lunging in with the bed sheet, Dad wraps the seal up tightly, it can no longer slap at him with its flippers but its doing its almighty best to take a chunk out of anything with those wicked teeth.

Dad picks up the baby seal keeping the teeth far from his face, "so what do you say we try to find a home for this guy?" "Wow," now we are all jumping with excitement! This seal goes from the dinner plate to the possibility of being rescued in a heartbeat. We have a mission; we are going to take off into the wild blue and incredibly vast yonder that stretches to the North Pole and find another seal's breathing hole to put this baby in! Not a problem, there is no sweat in the Arctic you know.

I get the first round. I sit on the front of the Komatik with my feet braced against the runners. I really don't want to do this. This snarly baby has now peed all over the bed sheet and he is intent on chewing on someone, I don't want it to be me. My Dad hands me the seal, he is heavy and feels like moving water in a fur bag. I am surprised at the weight. Jerking forward the skidoo lurches as it starts off.

I cannot hold on to the sled and hold on to this baby as well. The lead line is long to allow us to climb over ice chunks. Up we go, down we thump. I have no balance and this beast is taking every opportunity to try to bite me. His teeth catch in my parkie and he thrashes to get free. I am struggling to hold onto forty pounds of biting jello with razor teeth...oh yeah, he continues to pee on the bed sheet and me. I can hold on no more, I slide to the side and the skidoo comes to a stop.

Dad holds the ungrateful beast and my mother drives the skidoo. Unbelievable, directly in front of us in this endless land of ice and snow a black spot in the ice becomes apparent, truly out of nowhere. We slow down and watch as my father unwraps this trashing biting bundle of ultimate cuteness. The seal is in such a frenzy that it doesn't see his escape route He gets a nudge from a foot and slips away as if never there, silently into the liquid black. Not even a thank you, we walk away smiling, glad that this baby has another chance. Maybe David has fresh seal to share for supper tonight.

COPPERMINE

FLASH FROZEN

This is our last chance. Seams in the ice are cracking open and moving horizontally alongside the beaches in Coppermine, N.W.T located on the shores of the Arctic Ocean. It will be months until the sea ice is gone, but safety gets shifted in relevance to warmth. The warmer it gets, the less stable is the ice pack.

A week or more ago our family went out sealing (seal hunting) on this vast and frozen ocean. We rescued a baby seal that had wandered away from his frozen breathing hole. It is not easy transporting 40 pounds of biting Jell-O to a new home somewhere in the great unknown. Forget the needle in the haystack; we are searching for an open breathing hole on the wide-open expanses of the gigantic Arctic Ocean. Did I tell you, we did it? It was pretty groovy saving that baby.

All of our friends and neighbours heard our 'baby seal rescue' storey. It sounded like fun. Once it is over, bungee jumping is fun. However, it is a grand reason for almost 40 people to load up their Komatiks or miscellaneous carryalls and head out for a weekend on the sea ice…before the ice pack breaks up that is.

One by one off into the great white north we go. Sun shines, eyes squint, engine noise on skidoos rise and fall in volume as they climb up ice heaves and drop down over the other side. The odd kid gleefully falls off the family Komatik. It has been an unusually warm spring. We resemble an invasion.

People who have never travelled on the frozen ocean are included in this group as well as the regular adventurers. Teachers, Inuit and M.O.T. personal, Hudson Bay staff and more Inuit. An assortment of men, women and children go exploring in Canada's wilderness. We are Canadians; we do this sort of thing. This is not reality T.V., this is reality.

It is not often that a group this large travels together; several of my friends from school are on this trip. I am foolish, I want to be fashionable and groovy, I wear my gumboots. The black ones with the brick coloured accents. I even roll the tops down like the big girls do. Such gentle temperatures for this time of year, the thermometer soars up past freezing, the snow is mushy making it harder and harder for the skidoos to pull the heavy Komatiks across the frozen sea.

Hard working engines grind with the loads as they drag their weight through the heavy wet snow, seconds later the Komatiks are released from the mushy wet stuff as a clear patch of ice is exposed and the sleds break free and threaten to collide with the skidoos.

We resemble slingshots on ice, watching to make sure that limbs don't get squashed between the sled and the skidoo.

It is a winter carnival on the big whiteness. Tents are erected and kids chase one another around skidoos and empty sleds. Adults cheerfully call back and forth as they attempt to secure their canvas covers for the arctic night. Primus stoves (Coleman camp stoves) are our heat and cooking source. Camp is quickly constructed.

Being a speck on the huge expanse of sea ice intimidates some people. A sense of total vulnerability over whelms one of the ladies. This is her first time out on the frozen ocean. You are a speck in time, insignificance becomes apparent. I wonder if this is a same sensation that Blue Water Sailors experience. It is a release; you are so minute in this vast world, your problems and schemes become as insignificant as you are. They are really not worth worrying about or creating are they?

That is unless the temperature begins to plunge. Overnight a shift in the wind occurs. Gentle southern breezes swing over to fresh gusts from the north. My gumboots are now cold and clunky, even minutes after crawling out of my warm sleeping bag, sliding my warm feet into the frozen rubber takes seconds to suck the warmth out of small toes and my feet are very cold, I can say nothing. How silly is it to wear gumboots out camping?

Grownups are talking quietly, the men are standing in a group by the skidoos having a serious discussion, something is wrong. Quickly tents are taken down and Komatiks re-packed. Sleeping bags are left out, woman and children are wrapped in the sleeping bags and we are tied to the sleds. We have 30 miles to go to get to the safety of town.

With heads bowed for protection from the frozen gusts we begin our return journey. Gusts swing into blasts of blowing snow; we are being blown sideways by a whiteout. Hands in mittens are losing feeling as they grasp the ropes that secure us to the loads we are riding on. People sitting for long periods begin to freeze, we must stop. I have no feeling in my feet.

Tents are quickly erected. We only set up two tents and crowd people in for warmth. Primus stoves provide some heat and inside the shelter the temperature raises enough to prevent fingers and toes from freezing. I slide my feet into a sleeping bag beside my friend Grace, she looks at me with wide eyes when she feels how cold they are against her leg, she says nothing as well. What can you do? She moves in closer to make sure I am getting as much of her body warmth on my feet as possible.

Several of the Inuk men head out into the raging storm. They will return with the Bombardier to rescue us. Two dirty white canvas tents sit out exposed on the Arctic Ice. Blasting snow and bitter cold attempts to creep through the flaps. Swirling, biting and howling the furies chase each other around our shelters screaming in defiance. People on the outside edge change places with the people on the inside of the group to keep warm.

Sliced frozen caribou and red, red char are eaten raw with plenty of salt. Buckets of tea steam on the two burner stoves. Tea is thick, acid and black with lots of sugar. Pilot biscuits are handed out, rations need to be kept small, we don't know how long we will have to wait until we can get home. There is plenty of light in the spring of the year.

No sweat in the Arctic, no panic, cards are played and strings are pulled in games of "Cat's Cradle." We wait. Howling winds have slowed but the cold is dropping deeper. Tummy's growl and we wonder if there will be supper later. A frozen bannock is discovered by an older kid, of course we share. "Yuck", it has gas on it. We could light it on fire to heat up the tent; we are not hungry enough to eat it, yet. We keep it for a possible 'later.'

Faintly, faintly on the wind a sound comes and leaves again. Soon the strands of the song over the frozen sea remain connected, a steady low rumble that is climbing ice heaves and dropping off to a lower tone. Closer and closer, we hear our black steed approach. Laughing we know we will most probably sleep in a warm bed tonight and supper will be on the stove.

Of course, minor repairs need to be done to the Bombardier. They never travel far without parts falling off or busting loose. Inuk guys are magician mechanics. In the freezing, freezing cold with bare fingers on burning cold metal they work. A ski had worked itself loose, we are now free to go.

Crammed into the black box on tracks, sitting on hard as rock seats, we head off over ice heaves and snow. We are sitting two and three on top of each other, its fun if you are not the person sitting on the seat, on the bottom of the dog pile. Kids have no bones; we flop over and bounce down to the floor laughing like fools, such fun!

I am glad to be home, I am afraid to see my feet. There are many remedies for unthawing frozen person parts in the north. Put the frozen part in warm water, no wait, put it in cold water. My favourite, rub it with snow. Bare feet on snow is crazy. We do this as a challenge, my brothers and I. Who can run the farthest from the house on bare feet and back in the ice cold? Not today.

A bath would be a good idea after camping; it would not raise suspicions about my silliness. My feet in the warm bath water have begun to burn and itch. The itching is unbearable. Feeling is returning to my feet, I would have preferred them to remain blocks of ice. Ok, I guess I wait to see what will happen, I am afraid they will turn black and have to be cut off. We all know people who have had frozen parts cut off.

Several days later my feet begin to peel, Skin comes off in layers, mostly from the bottoms. I can wiggle my toes and bend my feet I have feeling in all of the parts. I am thirteen years old, I knew better when I was eight. Such foolishness is not acceptable; I will never do THAT again. This is the first time I have confessed to this, my dad will see it when he reads this paper and he will shake his head as he remembers his silly little girl.

P.S. This is the last trip that we took out on to the sea ice, the government will be moving us yet again.

COPPERMINE

THE NASAVAQ

(AN OLD BOAT)

Lying on the wind swept beach, a giant bank of snow has started to soften and reveal the outlines of a brooding hulk. A curve of ribs is displayed against the skyline. A dark splash begins to show on the rib line as the sun finds it attractive against the vast whiteness, the sun concentrates its warmth on the black spot and the blemish begins to grow. Slowly the black spot reaches the size of a dinner plate, it freezes at night and the process begins again the next day, the dinner plate becomes a dark platter as days lengthen. The nights are less frozen; the platter has now grown and become a curved black line drawn against a white horizon.

Sea ice begins to move and shift, in this old time it doesn't melt, it shifts. Most of the hulk is laying on open display amongst the rolled pebbles that make up this empty section of beach. Forty feet long with a depth of twelve feet, its black/grey body has not moved during the deep freeze of winter in the high Canadian Arctic. On the shores of the Arctic Ocean it lays awaiting its fate. The majority of the bay is clear; the tinkle of ice rotting in the sun comes from far in the distance. Summer has come and will last briefly.

A flash of colour signals the overnight bloom of wild flowers. Whirrling wings of ptarmigan startle children that are creeping over the tundra hunting lemmings. With summer jumping off of the sun in a swift and defiant motion, the birds are caught with some of their winter white plumage on. They appear to be half dressed in white vests and brown leggings, almost pulled up. Who wants to waste their time hunting lemmings, the child hunters are now in hot pursuit of "chickens".

Rumbles of a D-6 cat signal it's on a track toward the beach. This is time to move the large dark presence back to the Ocean. It moves with surprising ease. Pebbles are embedded in its sides as it is shoved toward the seashore. Out, out it is pushed, the sea creeps up and up, "good nuff, no more, we will drown it." With a slow bob the 40-foot bulk is floating. "Careful, where is the wobble pump?" Two men in gumboots hop onboard the listing Nasavaq. Long shafted hand pumps are stuck in her bowels. Steel tubes remove the saline solution from her hold. An 85 Horse diesel inboard engine cannot be submerged. A leak here, a leak there, back and forth the men work the hand crank on the pumps, creak, creak, creak, not a big deal…the old wooden ship sighs as her load is lightened within her aged frame. Will she live again?

With gentle movement she sits up right and surveys her bay. Coppermine, home of the Inuit (Eskimo) is where she lives. The Nasavaq is a 40-foot Government freighter. She has a beam of 12 feet and a flush deck for hauling freight. Below decks are the galley and 4 bunks; my father prefers to sleep by the engine to keep warm. In waters of liquid ice, it is never warm. The Nasvaq is used to freight fuel and grub to sealing camps during the summer. In the fall she hauls human cargo to Coppermine. School children from Holman Island are freighted in to stay with relatives over the winter so they can attend school.

Her cruising speed is 8 to 10 knots. With her jib and main sail she gains a few more knots depending on the winds, this also de-creases her fuel consumption. Built sometime in the 1930's she has been a dependable asset to the northern communities that surround Coppermine.

I lay on the flush deck (no rails) of the Nasavaq with my head hanging over the edge. Water so clear it is hard to tell if it is really there. Someone beside me spits, we all watch the frothy mix hit the water and cause a small ripple. It is real, we are on the Arctic Ocean so clean and clear that we can't believe it is really holding us up in this old wooden boat.

"That water is cold, if you fall over board you will be dead before we can turn around to get you." "Don't be stupid, don't fall overboard." We don't. Life jackets are referred to as body retrieval devices and nothing more. There are none on board. Seawater has to reach a temperature of -1.8c in order to freeze due to its mix of salt and water. This is liquid ice.

In the water I see millions upon millions of transparent white jellyfish. They are small, the size of a quarter or the very big ones like a 50-cent piece. (There were no loonies then) A bloom of these pulsing white transparencies dance their way toward the surface heading to a destination that I cannot see. There is no smell of brine and seaweed as there is on the pacific coast. I can see no fish, no shells, no sea cookies (sand dollars). Over all I find it no so entertaining. But the swell of the ocean is lulling and it would be easy to fall asleep on deck in the heat of the sun.

"OK, lets take her around." We are headed back to Coppermine. With the oil changed and all systems secured it is time for my Dad and his crew to sail to Holman Island to gather the kids for school. "Can I go?" "No." There is barely room for the kids that have to make the return trip and the numbers can change at the last minute. Everyone has to fit down into the hold; there are no rails for security. If the seas came up it would be impossible to stay on deck without being swept over board into the Arctic Sea.

I think about stowing away, it is a hard decision. The humiliation of being disciplined in front of the other kids determines that this time I won't hide behind the engines, maybe next time. With a heavy sigh I climb down into the waiting boat that will take me ashore.

More kids are arriving back from summer camps every day. School will start soon. The older kids have already left for Akaitcho Hall in Yellowknife, others for Stringer Hall in Inuvik. Most Inuit are of Anglican faith they attend different residential schools than the Dene of the McKenzie River. The Catholic Church does not structure their residential schools. School goes to grade eight here, it only went to grade six in Fort Good Hope. The older kids are, 'glad to go back to civilization.' They are getting used to the lights of the big cities of Yellowknife and Inuvik.

We get to try something new this year. We will go to school from 12 noon until 5 p.m. During the Polar Night we get no sun in December and January and barely dusk in November and February. This is to help make it easier for the little kids to get to school. My friend Grace's Uncle Allen has a rope that he ties around his waist in the winter. He has knots tied all along it and we have to hold on at the knots until we get to the school doors. This works really well if we get caught in a whiteout. I always wondered what would happen to us if he got lost, but he never did.

Mrs. Grace Priest lives here now. I know her from Fort Norman; she is the Pentecostal Missionary that taught me how to knit with spikes. She will be teaching girl guides this year, she wants us to learn how to do British Marching Drills. We have high-class visitors coming here and they will need to see that we are good kids.

P.S. Hi everyone, I hope you had a great summer. Our summer was filled with a mix of blessings and challenges. I thought that I could write about the challenges, but I struggle with the reality of committing such things to paper. They become real to me when I do and I am just not ready for that. This is my 'round about apology for getting back in the saddle so late. I do have some very exciting projects that I will be sharing with you this winter. So here we go, I am ready to settle into a winter of sharing the White Girl Series with you…and thank you, for all of your support it is really important. Mashi dwai.

COPPERMINE

VISITORS OF DISTINCTION

"NO WAY!"'Sh-h-h…really, don't scare him.' Perched precariously over the stinky dark depths of the honey bucket (ancient disposable toilet) is Sam the Siamese cat, my cat. He responds to our intrusion with an icy stare of distain as only a cat can do. Rather than Sam being embarrassed at being caught in this position of privacy, we feel shamed by our lack of manners and consideration.

Poor critter, there is no litter box when it is forty below in the ice and snow. This is before kitty litter graced back porches with claims of being odor free. No one could ever imagine letting a pet poop inside, are you serious! Sam had to claw through frozen drifted snow to attend to his business…and keep a third eye open for sled dogs that would love a kitty dinner.

Under our propped-up house there is rock and frozen hard gravel that he could at least make a show of covering up his leavings. It drives him crazy to leave uncovered evidence of his poop (if only the dogs felt the same). Snow has drifted in and covered his access to beneath the house, he is at his wits end, the only thing left is the honey bucket. He is a brave, brave cat!

Sam has recently been caught eating the cigarette ashes out of the ash-tray and licking up dry dark crystals of instant coffee that have escaped onto the counter. He is not allowed on the counter, this is double jeopardy. We watch him from the hallway; he daintily licks up the coffee crystals sticks out his tongue in disgust but continues to eat. Giggles cause him to look up and he makes a dash for the door; he must be needing something more to eat than caribou meat.

"Left, left…right and now quadrille"! All winter long we have been marching, turning and keeping count.Mrs. Grace Priest is the Pentecostal missionary in Coppermine, N.W.T. She calls us her 'Soldiers of God. 'We, the Girl Guides of Canada have been preparing this marching demonstration north of the Arctic Circle on the shores of the Arctic Ocean.

We will be presenting our drill to the Governor General of Canada, the Honourable Roland Michener and his wife, the Lady Norah Michener.

Our guests are due to arrive next week, the community is buzzing with excitement. We are nervous; we want our performance to be perfect. Plans are in place that includes an expedition for the Governor General to fish for Char at Bloody Falls; Mrs. Michener will have a social tea at our house.

Bloody Falls is located on the Coppermine River just over the knoll and a few more miles from the village of Coppermine. Bloody Falls was site of a massacre on July 17th, 1771. Chipewyan and Dene Indians, part of Samuel Hearne's exploration party, fell on and killed approximately 20 Eskimo men, women and children. It was declared a Canadian National Historic Site in 1978.

Arctic Char thrive in the flowing liquid ice of the Coppermine River. Such a beautiful fish, slips of silver flash in the crystal cold waters. The meat of this Char is firm and deep, dark red in colour, a signature colour of Char found beneath the Bloody Falls. Char is a delicate tasting fish. We would eat it frozen, shaved off with an axe and sprinkled with salt. Smoked Char is wonderful as well; I never had this delicacy until I moved back below the tree line, where there is alder wood for fish smoking.

A day before the distinguished couple is to appear, special items show up flown in by a DC 3 airplane from Yellowknife, N.W.T.Fresh lemons, fresh oranges, our freezer has been filled with frozen Sara Lee cakes of all flavours, and cheesecakes?? Frozen cream puffs, can you imagine? We just can't help ourselves!

One little cake won't be missed when there are so many...running till our lungs bust, we race to hide behind the black rocks way-y-y out in the backyard. Out comes the suddenly very small box that contains a Sara Lee pound cake. Ten kids bite chunks from this so very tiny cake. 'Ever eat cheese cake, sounds grody!' 'Nope, you?' 'We should try it, there are tons of them in the freezer.' "Ok, 'whos 'goin?' Send Kurtie this time, he's little, they won't see him.' 'If I go I'll get stuck doin dishes.'

Kurt comes back in a flash with a cake AND a cheesecake under his coat. 'Take a bite!' 'You first, who puts cheese in cake?" 'Weird white-eyes from the south.' 'Ha, ha, I'll eat it if don't want it!' Now we all want a chunk of this cake that tastes like sour ice cream. Melting cheesecake and graham crumbs are licked off of fingers with young faces smiling in ecstasy. I have one more treat in my pocket.

I have a real lemon.'Want to try?' Eyebrows are raised in the sign for yes...eyebrows are lowered if you mean no, body language is important, how can you talk to someone if you can't see them? The lemon is peeled into sections like an orange...faces scrunch into sour pusses. These kids have never had a fresh lemon. Cake is good but lemon is magnificent! We only have the one lemon to share, they are closely guarded, they are precious.

Mrs. Michener will be hosting a community tea at our house. All of the remaining cakes and cream puffs will be served at the social. Mrs. Michener likes fresh lemon in her tea. All ladies in Coppermine are invited to attend, and they do. Special china teacups in scripted with the N.W.T crest are provided, the cups and saucers feel like egg shells, I am careful as I wash them.

Mrs. Michener has a tremble in her hands. She has her tea in a cup with no saucer; the coffee table is placed close in front of her so if she wishes to set her cup down she can do so without dropping it.With her tremble the teacup would rattle on the saucer and cause her embarrassment. We are not sure why she would be embarrassed, it is how she is and she is a very nice lady, we like her.

She chats with all of the women, asking them real questions, she waits patiently for real answers, she wants to hear what the women have to say, she does not pretend interest, she is interested.

Sam the Siamese cat comes slinking into the room and dives under the coffee table.I look up with concern. I cannot get under the table to get him without causing a ruckus and appearing to be looking up Mrs. Michener's dress, what to do?

Sam was once lost on the Bear River, west of Fort Norman for months, the last barge of the year found him on the rivers bank eating a duck that he had killed. The Bargemen have great difficulty capturing this miniature wild cat. He never lost his sense of newfound wildness and hated having strangers in his house. Launching himself off the top of fridge onto an unsuspecting visitor was his glory; we always locked him up when company showed up. He has escaped.

This wonderful lady spies him and comments that she has two of her own Siamese Cats at home. While she is sharing this with us she reaches down with her very vulnerable and frail hand to scratch the demons ears. In a hissing heartbeat he swings a full on attack with claws failing in fury, how dare she touch 'him'? Oh god, my cat has just scratched this really, really nice lady who is also the wife of the Governor General of Canada, again, what to do!

Blood flows quickly from the scratches of the delicate skin on the back of her hand. "It is alright, I am quite fine," she insists. My mom has brought a clean cloth, bandages and hydrogen peroxide to help treat the hurt. Mrs. Michener says that one of the reasons she enjoys her cats so much is their high spirits. I have never heard of bad manners and wildness referred to as 'high spirits', Sam is locked in the back bedroom.

We take turns walking with the Governor General in the morning. Six of the Girl Guides have been chosen to accompany him on his morning walk. Roland Michener is a good man. He also asks us questions that he expects answers to. A grown up is asking what we would do to help our community…and he really wants to know what we think. 'What are the problems that you face? ''How do you think we can fix things?'

I have been approached in this time, by politicking politicians with questions on my thoughts for my community. More often than not, they then tell me what I am thinking or if I do get the opportunity to speak, their eyes glaze over and I believe they are considering what 's for dinner because they certainly are not listening to what I have to say. Their obligation of implied interest has been met by asking the question, they seldom care for the reply.

I feel privileged to be asked what I am thinking by this very important man. I tell him what I think without reserve. He listens intently, he doesn't once say that I am only a kid and don't know what I am talking about. We walk together toward the shores of the Arctic Ocean, dust clouds puff around our feet; my new shoes are new no more. This man reminds me of my far away grandfather. He stops and takes my hand; he says "I believe that in your lifetime you will contribute greatly to your community and Canada will be proud of you."

Kids were seen and not to be heard in this time, he actually listened to me.I take his every word and paste it directly on to my heart. In following years, times were hard raising two children by myself. Those days when you wonder 'what in the hell am I doing, and am I really doing it right', I would take out Roland Michener's words, shake them off, rev them up and carry on. Be careful what you say to children, they often paste your words directly on to their hearts.

COPPERMINE

HEADING INTO THE SUNSET

Roy

Giving up my paper route is not hard. There are few jobs for young people in this far and away section of Canada's True North. Allen Niptanatiak is happy to take over the weekly delivery of News of the North for me. (Now called News/North) A scheduled flight by Twin Otter on Fridays drops off the packet of 22 newspapers. I start out with 12 papers and have increased my clientele to 22. The News of the North arrives via air from Yellowknife, NWT. The pay is not worth fighting blinding snowstorms and freezing fingers, but my customers love the anomaly of having their paper delivered to their doors at the edge of the mostly frozen Arctic Ocean, they tip very well.

We are moving west into the setting sun. Our new home will be in the almost new town of Inuvik. Inuvik becomes the first and only town north of the Arctic Circle in 1970; we arrive in the winter of 1971. On July 21, 1961Prime Minister John Diefenbaker officiated at a dedication ceremony in the then village of Inuvik. The unveiling of a plaque declared Inuvik to be the first community north of the Arctic Circle built to provide the normal facilities of a Canadian town. Wow, we have been living in abnormal circumstances, nobody told us. What is normal exactly?

What is terrible hard, is giving up our dogs. We will be living in a town, sharing half of one those brightly coloured duplexes with another family. The houses are all grouped together to accommodate the utilidors that supply houses with water and carry the sewage to some other place. Utilidors are built several feet off the frozen ground, an insulated corridor constructed of steel and aluminum. The absolute perfect kid freeway. Of course we are not allowed to use these steel highways, but we do. There is no room in town for dog team storage.

Our boys are leaving home. We have known them since birth. Snuggling in close to their warm baby breath we were tolerated by their loving mother as each pup was turned with professional curiosity to see if they are boy or girl puppies. They are baby boys; my dad has his new team of dogs!

The boys were born and trained in Fort Good Hope. Travelling beside the old dog team, they struggled with their fat baby bellies to keep up with the giant, slow moving freighter dogs that were my father's first dog team. Stumbling in the snow with little pink tongues rolling in doggy smiles, they loved the run.

Growing into adolescence their lanky legs and bondless energy makes it difficult for Dad to get them into the tracers. "Let's go, let's go, come on you slow man, lets get on the trail!" Jumping, barking and flipping in their harness, Dad gets one untangled just in time to untangle yet another exhilarated dog.

The sleigh is tied to the shed, the brake has been set, my dad stands on the brake and quickly wraps the rope around his hand. Shooting like grey hounds from the start gate at a race track, the brake slows them only a little. Rooster tails of snow shoot out the signal that dad has hit the trail. Flat out dog power whips him around the shed and he is gone, headed for the Mackenzie River. "Haw, Haw." My dad commands, he is enjoying the speed and frenzied excitement as much as his 'boys' are.

Our dog team were then flown from below the tree line on the McKenzie River in the N.W.T. Canada to Coppermine located on the shores of the Arctic Ocean. There are no trees to pee on here. Their home in Fort Good Hope was a wired in dog pen/run where they were individually chained. They look a little bewildered being tied to a long line of chain with no trees in site, where are the trails?

We feel as displaced as they do. Grabbing a ruff of fur we pet and roll them on their backs, we have grown up together. Ace, the lead dog is at the end of the dog run, we give him a clear berth. His bulging blind eye lends little to his already threatening demeanor, he came to us late in his life, we don't like him, he has chewed on our baby brother..

From narrow snow shoed trails through pecker pine poles to the wide-open vistas of arctic sea, these are well-travelled dogs. There is no room for them and the new life style that we are travelling to in Inuvik N.W.T

How do you give away your friends and companions of many years? Sandy was the mother of the five "boys" who were the core of our dog team. Tippy was the father of the team. Ace was the lead dog, I was fine with leaving him, he had chewed up my baby brother Kurtis. That storey is called 'Biting the Hand that Feeds You' and can be viewed and purchased at Kobo.com under The White Girl title.

What to do? We had crawled into the doghouse with Sandy while she was giving birth to the boys. Rolling them around on their fat baby bellies and listening to them growl at us with sharp voices, how can we leave them? We watched as Dad trained them to follow along side the Old Freighter dogs that were his first team. They would fall on their faces in the deep snow, so happy to be running down the trail. They learned from the example of these gentle giant dogs to be the very best dog team.

Their first run in the tracers! Such excitement, jumping and leaping in the air! Flipping over the tracers and harness causing an impossible tangle of lines and hooks. Doggy smiles with tongues flopping sideways in happiness, 'lets go Master, let us take you into the wild!" "Hurry, hurry you are much too slow Master, let us run!" "Come with us, let us run!" My poor Dad would get them untangled just to have them jump over the tracers and it began all over again.

Such a beautiful team of matched brothers, Shorty, Roy, Charlie…on special occasions they wore their embroidered blankets complete with fringed stroud and bells. Ace sported an adornment that sat 8 inches above his head made with pom poms of colourful wool, attached ribbons flew in the breezes the team created with their haste. Blue eyed Siberian Huskies, shades of amber to black on white, they were stunning. Their smiling eyes carried over into their turned up lips in a grimace of smiles they must have inherited from their mother Sandy.

We have a mystery. I recently talked to May Gudmundson. She and her husband Brian spent many years in the north. Brian was with the R.C.M.P. I believe that May was a school teacher. May said that they ended up with Tippy, Ace and Sandy while they lived in Aklavik, when we moved to Inuvik.

Tippy was renowned for his hatred of other dogs, he was the perfect wheel dog, always wanting to take a chunk out of the furry butt in front of him…the momentum kept the sled flying! Sandy was his sweetheart. Not long after Gudmundsons adopted our dogs, Sandy came into heat and Tippy engaged in battle. The battle resulted in him being wounded. The wounds soon were infected and became mortal, Tippy travelled on to the big dog sled in the sky.

Sandy gave birth to four more pups while in Aklavik with the Gudmundsons. After the pups were born May noticed a large lump in Sandy's breast area. Surgery needed to be done. Dr. Dave McQuarrie was to perform the surgery on the Gudmundson's kitchen table. He decided that Sandy would require more anesthetic than he had on hand; she was shipped to the hospital in Inuvik. Dr. McQuarrie laid claim to one of Sandy's pups.

Brian Gudmundson was in the hospital in Inuvik having been burnt in an explosion in a garage that then caught on fire. He called and asked my Dad if we would be able to take care of Sandy, Brian is needing time to recover from his burns. My Dad was ecstatic to have Sandy back. She was my brother John's dog and our family pet. We had moved to a larger house, with an individual yard that could accommodate Sandy and Sam the wild Siamese cat as well.

I watch as my parents carry Sandy inside the house on a blanket after her surgery. She barely moves her head she is so heavily drugged. Her lips lift in an attempt to show her teeth in an unmistakable Sandy smile, she falls into a deep sleep, we have her back, she is ours once again.

Dr. Dave McQuarrie sends in a biopsy of the lump removed from Sandy. The specimen is labeled simply as 'Sandy Gudmundson.' Instead of the usual three-week wait, a response comes quickly by phone. "This is most unusual, we have never come across a female sample with so many hair follicles." I don't know if the lab was ever told that Sandy Gudmundson was a dog. The diagnosis is that it is cancer.

Sandy died five years later in Whitehorse. She became part of our family in Fort Norman, NWT in 1966; she ran into our house in Crestview and fell dead on the floor possibly from a heart attack in 1977. My brother John's friend Kenny Olson was babysitting her at the time. It was a tough spot to be in Kenny. She had a wonderful life, travelling more than most people of that era. She was never treated for cancer. One of her eyes was blue the other eye brown with a fleck of white, she had a beautiful smile.

Ace our lead dog continued on to Sachs Harbour, NWT with the Gudmundsons. He had been a retired R.C.M.P. dog when we inherited him in Fort Good Hope in 1968. From Coppermine he travels to Aklavik, then Fort McPherson and finally to Sachs. When he became too old to keep up as lead dog he insists he can run along side the team. Once a leader always a leader, he would cause a commotion by trying to remain boss, he could not stand being left behind, like all of the sled dogs we know, he loved to be on the trail.

On a sunshiny day in springtime Ace fell asleep on the roof of his doghouse. He never woke up. May said she mentioned to Brian "Ace hasn't moved in a few hours." Brian went out to check on him. May saw Brian take Ace in his arms and she knew he was gone. Ace lies under a cairn of rocks on Banks Island NWT.

The mystery. My dad is sure that Brian and May took the whole team, (all eight dogs) sled, harness and dog shoes. May remembers only getting three dogs. I have not talked to Brian yet. (I am looking forward to hearing his version, May's was exceptional) I have no memory what so ever of what happened to our pups. I have blocked traumatic events in my life, this may be another.

I don't remember the pups flying with us in the DC3 airplane that moves us to Inuvik. I have been afraid until today to ask where the pups went in the event that they were sent prematurely to dog sled heaven as well. It was a reality of those times. There were no animal shelters, should we set them lose and let them starve? When I find out what became of the pups I will let you know. The elusive thought in the recesses of my memory is Colin Adjun, the famous Inuit fiddler laid claim to the boys and they remained to run the tundra of the Arctic?

P.S. The absolute greatness of stories is that we all have our own. In the north we celebrate individualism, who wants to be like everyone else? Thank you to May for her input, she has an amazing memory and a hundred or more stories that need to be told. Both May and Brian live in Whitehorse as does my father.

INUVIK

THE TOWN OF INUVIK

Inuvik became the first and only town in Canada, north of the Arctic Circle in 1970. It was the largest military base in the north with a population of over 250 Military personnel and a combined population that included personnel families that reached approximately 700 in total. A combination of Eskimo and Indian and White peoples placed population figures around 3,000 people. This sanctioned Town is situated above the Arctic Circle and just 70 miles below the shores of the Icy Beaufort Sea.

Inuvik means "The Place of Man". A melting pot of race, religion and oil exploration. This town was further north than there were roads, if you were to travel here you arrived by boat or plane only. For a young White Girl, the combination of language, race and customs were incomprehensible.

INUVIK

INUVIK: THE PLACE OF MAN

Inuvik, in 1971 is the first and only town north of the Arctic Circle built to provide the normal facilities of a Canadian town. This is not a town, this is a city, this place has a grocery store! You can't walk down the centre of the road; the cars and trucks will hit you. We have to learn new rules about walking on the road or they honk and scare us. There are no dog bells on dog teams anymore; there are horns on vehicles. Everybody has a phone at their house, can you believe it? Still no T.V.

Inuvik has a movie theatre with funny seats that slide up and down. At the little store beside the theatre you buy peanut butter milkshakes. They make them with powered milk; the peanut butter covers up the taste of the Klim pretty well. (Brilliance in marketing, Klim is milk spelled backwards, they should have worked on the taste factor instead). Across the street is a bakery. Pastries are lined up behind the glass. Filled with raspberry or strawberry jam, they melt in your mouth. Tri-milk is new to us. A liter of frozen tri-milk is thawed out and diluted with two liters of water. It makes drinkable milk!

Inuvik has town kids, residential kids and Military kids. Segregation within the residences are; Catholic Indians in Grollier Hall, and Stringer Hall is for the Eskimo Anglicans. This is a puzzle. Friends that I grew up with on the Deh Cho (Mackenzie River) are in the Catholic residence; friends from the Arctic coast are in Stringer Hall, they all kept separate.

The churches and the government segregate everyone. How can everyone be friends if they keep separating all of us into specific groups? Each group is assigned different rules and has different privileges. They say we are all the same, but each group gets different treatment; of course people get angry when the rules are not fair, or they change depending on who you are. It doesn't matter to me what church kids go to or what language they speak, they are still my friends. What are the church and the government doing with this segregation thing? Segregation is separation, divide and conquer.

Town kids and the military kids have different rules as well. The Military kids are regulated even more, they have commanders for fathers. There is no level playing field. Fights break out between the town kids and the military kids. You need to know who you can hang out with and who you can't? I don't know what to do, I want to play volleyball and listen to new music at T.O.A.S.T. (a teen club where they actually make us toast) with my friend Leslie Carpenter. Summer will be here soon, I will be able to ride a bike and play baseball on a real baseball field, I can hardly wait! But in the meantime…

I can see in some of the white girl's eyes that they don't like me, but they still smile with their mouths and say hello very sweetly. Why do they do that? They have no honour in pretending to like me when they don't. Why would they be such hypocrites, you can't even tell who your friends really are. My friends from the Deh Cho and the Arctic Coast now live in residence, it is not cool for them to hang out with a white town kid, I am in no man's land in this 'place of man'.

My northern 'accent' is strong compared to these white kids. Living on the Deh Cho, my English has been slanted by the song of Slavey and after life on the Arctic Coast I have undertones of Inuk. I have been asked if I am from Ireland in more present years, surprising to me and probably to the Irish as well. It is a strange tongue I speak, conversations are salted with Slavey 'swear' words and little 'goomuks' (bugs) of Inuk. It is fun to switch between three languages, the teachers are confused.

We have been in the theater to watch 'Kelly's Heroes'; it was a popular movie last year on the outside. It is a cold and black night. The few streetlights illuminate blowing snow coming down hard. My friends live on the other side of town, we say good-night, I walk towards the Lady of Victory Catholic Church (the famous Igloo Church of Inuvik) an attempt to short cut my way home. My head is down to avoid the snow; I trip over a bundle in the snow and turn to go around it. It looks like ragged clothes that someone has dropped in a pile.

Something is wrong, I stop. There is something in the pile of clothes. I could feel it when I kicked it with my foot. Oh my, I have to go back and look. I don't want to look; I don't know what I will find. What if it's a body? What is it's a chewed up body that the dogs left? What if it's a body with the head cut off? I am thirteen years old; my imagination is running wild, I have just watched Kelly's Heroes! I am terrified!

Cautiously I return to the bundle of rags that now looks like a person since I am paying attention. Snow covers the pile; I slowly put out my hand to push the rags. It is solid, it is a person! What to do? This person could be alive, if I run for help it might be too late, nothing is open this late at night, there is no one around.

I push hard on the pile, it moves. I don't know if I am more scared or happy! He falls over with a moan. My god it's Tommy, I know Tommy from when we were little. Now I can smell the booze on him, I have to get him to somewhere warm. He lives in the Catholic residence, he will be in so much trouble if I take him home, but he might live.

He mumbles 'leave me be'. 'I can't you will die, your brother will kill me', I say. I want to say 'I might kill you Tommy, for being so stupid!' Now I am getting mad. 'Tommy you jerk!' 'Try to walk!' 'Leave me be white girl, I want to sleep.' I pull him by the hair; he doesn't like that and tries to grab me. Good, there is life in him yet! He is up on his knees, he has only a light shirt on no jacket, I don't have much time. The sleep of frozen death is an easy call to accept.

I get his arm over my shoulder, 'give me a lil' kiss'. 'Shut up you pig, I am going to kick you in the balls if you don't start to move!' He knows I mean it. Stumbling in the snow and wind he wobbles on his skinny legs. Thank god he is a skinny little guy. We drag/ walk, fall and crawl towards Grollier Hall. I am freezing; my fingers numb from holding Tommy tight. He is on his knees once again, he whimpers, 'I can't go home, I'm drunk!'

'Too bad,' I say, 'I have nowhere else to take you and it's better than if you freeze to death.' 'What would your family say if I let you freeze?' He really doesn't want to go back to residence at this point and slumps to the ground. I am losing him. I grab his shirt at the shoulders and drag him through the snow. He mumbles swear words at me trying to kick his feet to slow us down. I am pretty strong and he is fairly light, adrenalin pushes me forward. I drag him up the stairs letting his feet bump behind him. Dropping him at the top of the stairs I pound on the door. Lights come on.

'What's this, what are you doing girl!' 'I brought Tommy home.' 'I have to go I am going to be in trouble for being late.' 'You are going nowhere girl, I am calling the RCMP you are drunk,' storms Father Ryant. 'I am not!' I exclaim. I found Tommy in the snow bank and I brought him home. I don't want him to know that I have been at the show, it was restricted to 14 years and older, I lied about my age I am only 13. My parents will kill me when they find out that I lied.

'You remain here until the RCMP arrive,' he turns and motions to people from the residence to take Tommy inside. Tommy is completely limp at this point. I stand frozen on the step waiting for the police. Father Ryant is mumbling about the 'town' kids corrupting his kids, how the town kids get away with everything and his kids get into trouble.

'I don't drink, I am not drinking,' I repeat. I can see that it makes no difference. The RCMP arrives in their steel steed. I am not afraid, I have done nothing wrong. I wait for them to talk to me. Father Ryant is ranting that they need to put me in jail. The RCMP walks me over to the car. It is so nice and warm in the back seat. Thank goodness, my feet are so, so cold. 'How are you doing?' the officer asks me. 'I am frozen,' I say.

'Were you drinking tonight?' 'No way, I just found Tommy and brought him home, he was freezing.' 'You did the right thing,' are you alright?' The tears come, 'I didn't think I was going to make it, I thought he would freeze and die!' 'I want to go home, I am in trouble.' 'You won't be in trouble,' the officer assures me.

My parents are amazed to see their daughter brought home in a police car. The RCMP explains the situation. My dad's mouth gets tight, he is not happy, but he is not mad at me for sure. I don't want to talk about this to anyone. I am embarrassed that Father Ryant said I was drunk. I hope that Tommy is OK, I am not sure that I like this big town. I don't understand these people; I want to go home, I want to go back to Fort Good Hope.

P.S. Tommy lived through this night. On this note I leave you for the summer. www.thewhitegirl.ca returns in the fall. Thank you all for your incredible support. If you need a White Girl or an Adventure of the Audrey Eleanor fix over the summer, you can go to Kobo.com and download any of my stories onto your phone, PC or e-reader for only $1. I have great pictures of the Audrey Eleanor on the white girl site. Have a great summer; remember there is NO SWEAT IN THE ARCTIC! Mashi

INUVIK

CAMP OF A CANNIBAL

WARNING; THIS ARTICLE CONTAINS GRAPHIC CONTENT, THIS IS REAL AND THIS IS HARSH. THIS IS TALK OF CANNIBALISM.

We have a new pilot touching down in swirls of snow, blowing into our town of Coppermine, N.W.T., Canada. Martin Hartwell comes to our house for coffee. Most everyone comes to our house for coffee. Mr. Hartwell ruffles our hair as he passes through the house and asks how we are doing with his strong German accent. He is one of the few pilots that acknowledges us kids.

Martin Hartwell is soon to become the centre of great focus around the world. On November 8th, 1972 he crashes his "Beech" 18 while on a Mercy flight to Yellowknife, N.W.T. He is on route from Cambridge Bay NWT, (now known as Nunavut) to Yellowknife with three passengers on board.

The three passengers are from Spence Bay, N.W.T. Canada. Neemee Nulliayok is eight months pregnant and experiencing complications. David Pisurayak Kootook is suffering from appendicitis, David and Neemee are Eskimo. Judy Hill, originally from Great Britain is the government nurse escorting these patients to Stanton Hospital in Yellowknife.

Experiencing bad weather and low cloud, the plane crashes into a long hillside near Hottah Lake, south of Great Bear Lake. Judy Hill is killed on impact; she is thrown forward onto Hartwell and partially threw his window. Neemee Nulliayok dies a short while later. David Kootok is alive. Hartwell has two broken ankles; his nose is fractured, as is his left knee. David is fourteen years old and in pain from appendicitis. He takes care of Martin Hartwell.

Temperatures average -35F. David erects a tent and attempts to keep a fire burning so they don't freeze. They are a long distance from Hotta

Lake; it expends much energy to gather firewood and chop through three feet of ice to try to catch a fish. David is done; he must have been exhausted from the cold and pain. They have had little food and emergency rations are gone. Martin decides that they need to eat part of Judy Hill if they wish to live. There is no way that he can crawl to the lake to fish. How could you crawl any distance with two broken ankles?

David apparently refuses to eat any of the nurse. We were so angry with him. Our grade nine class is paying close attention to this plane crash. Everyone waits to hear some news; everyday we wait for something to come over the airwaves on CBC saying that the people on the plane are alive. He is 14 years old, my classmates in Inuvik (we live in Inuvik in 1972) are 14 years old, we have formed a kinship with this missing teen, some of his family are related to someone else's family, that's how it is in the north, we are all one family. Everyday we waited.

Oh no, they called off the search, it is only three weeks, they could still be alive! Controversy runs like lightening through the moccasin telegraph. They say it has been too cold and no beacon has set off, they must be dead. But what if they aren't?

We don't know much about Martin Hartwell, he is a German from Europe, what would he know about surviving on the rock, snow and pecker pole studded barren lands of that area? Judy Hill, the nurse is from Britain, would she know anymore than the pilot…two Inuit would know what to do. But one is very pregnant and sick and the other is really just past being a boy and he has appendicitis, the odds are not good.

The search is resumed. We find out that David dies 20 days into the crash. Why on would he not eat part of the nurse? Martin Hartwell cut meat off of her leg to eat to survive. We are northern children; we are realists, why on earth wouldn't David decide to live? Fury mounts in the classroom as we probe and prod and pick at the wound that David's death has inflicted on all of us.

Martin Hartwell survives 31 days of pure hell on some of gods most frozen and desolate wasteland. Inquest and inquiry are technical difficulties that you may study for yourselves if you are inclined. Judy Hills mother said that she was sure that her daughter would be happy contributing to others in death, as she had in life.

People of the north shrugged shoulders at the consumption of human flesh in this life and death situation. When Search and Rescue found Martin Hartwell, his first words to them were" welcome to the camp of a cannibal."

Do you want to live? Or do you want to die? Personally I don't intend to hang around a decaying body once my life is done. I believe that I will have better things to do. I am gone, do what you will with the shell…if someone needs parts to live, you have my blessing to take what you like.

A year earlier, 1971 in Coppermine I experience deep burning pains in my right side. I think its just a stich from running too much or too fast. It doesn't go away. All night long the pain gets worse, I can't breathe, I am getting scared. The nurse at the nursing station decides that I have acute appendicitis. I am to be flown on a mercy flight to Stanton hospital in Yellowknife as soon as a plane can be had.

Martin Hartwell is the pilot that flies in to save me. My mother and I are flown to Yellowknife in a small plane, I don't know if it was the same Beech 18. I do remember his words with a thick German accent saying, "everything will be alright." The pain is receding. I find if I stay really, really still and take shallow breathes I can hold back the tears.

An ambulance speeds us off to the hospital. There is only one Doctor available. No one can find the Doctor. Nurses are 'fluttering moths' around my bedside; I assure them that I am not feeling as bad as I did in the morning. "Where is the Doctor, where is the Doctor,' has become a mantra in the operating room. He is also the anesthesiologist.

He enters the room on the whoosh of a whiskey front. "Oh my," exclaims a young nurse and then, complete silence. "Whada we got here?" the Doc slurs. My mother says, "You are drunk!" "You will not be operating on my daughter, get someone else." There is no one else. I am trying not to interrupt the adults, but I am thinking that I don't want this wobbly guy cutting into my guts!

"I 'm getting way better," I manage to squeak, "maybe we can just go home, I really do feel better." In a huff the Doctor departs, the fluttering nurses are now droning Bees, what do you do when the only Doctor in town is drunk? Well I think I like to keep my parts intact. For whatever reason, I feel much better, we can go home now.

We get to stay in the only hotel in town at the time, the Gold Range, known fondly to Northerners as the "Strange Range." There is a restaurant, I have a glass of real milk and a piece of Boston cream pie, and it is so good! .

I never did get my appendixes out; I have them to this day. I have no idea what the pain was, my suspicion is possibly a pulled muscle or a bruised rib; life was rough in 'them days.' Our nurse was being cautious, this is a good thing.

P.S. ....I wish that David have lived, it truly seems that the good do die young. He received many awards posthumously for his bravery in helping to keep Martin Hartwell alive, he would have been a good person to keep around, we need all of the good 'ones' that we can get. There were rumours of a note found in David's pocket written in Inuit. What the note said I do not know. This happened forty years ago on December 12, 1972.

INUVIK

WE HAVE BEEN CIVILIZED

Om nom nom nom, du doo du doo du, om nom nom nom, du doo doo du. Television has arrived in Inuvik, N.W.T. We have four hours of 'canned' T.V. every night starting at 6 p.m. The first hour is Sesame Street.

The Cookie Monster is a huge hit at Samuel Hearne Secondary School. Om nom nom nom (the Cookie Monster theme song at that time) is heard throughout the hallways with good and bad imitations of Cookie's gruff voice bouncing around in narrow spaces. Outsiders from the south watching SHSS grade 12 students singing Sesame Street songs would have shook their heads in wonder. It is all relevant, considering that they on the outside were singing Chuck Berry's song 'My ding-a-ling'!

After Sesame Street comes M.A.S.H, the streets clear in a mad rush as kids scramble to get home in time to watch M.A.S.H. M.A.S.H. becomes an over night sensation. How quickly our world has changed. Only a week ago we were in the school gym practicing layups or ponging the badminton birdie, now we dash for M.A.S.H.

Saturday night is Hockey Night in Canada! There is only one hockey game a week and everyone crowds around an available T.V. to watch. There are few T.V.s in Inuvik at this time. Slow and painful death is threatened to anyone who hints at the final outcome of Saturday night's game. If you had travelled from the outside or heard the news of last week's game from the south you would already have this information. Our T.V. is a taped week old version from the south; these games have already been won or lost. On Sundays, we simply can't miss watching the Beachcombers.

Volleyball is a serious sport, competition is fierce. Come to think of it, competition in any sport is fierce. I watch in wonder as Laura Sorensen travels the full length of the basketball court in seconds, jumps and taps the ball into the hoop like it was an everyday accomplishment. For her it is! I would not want to try to stop her.

The junior girls volleyball team is going to Aklavik for a tournament. This is a competition to see who will represent the Inuvik area in the upcoming Arctic Winter Games. I will be going to Aklavik to play with the Inuvik volleyball team.

We are flown over in a twin Otter and have to sleep on the floor of the gym. We are all nervous to be playing against these tough girls from Aklavik and Fort MacPherson (MacFoo). Moose stew is the food of gatherings. It can be kept hot and is easy to serve. We have moose stew for lunch and moose stew for supper. Someone makes incredible bannock. There is canned butter and strawberry jam, we eat more than our fair share of bannock, the moose stew smells like old rutting bull.

This competition is tough, these girls are deadly. They slam the volleyball in a spike that causes us to run and duck for our lives, instead of the interception we are supposed to be doing. Aint' nothin' worth gettin' your head taken off for. We are soon out of the competition and become tourists in this tiny hamlet.

This is the final resting place of the Famous Mad Trapper of Rat River. Walking over the Mad Trappers grave brings up our level of confidence again; we are not total chickens after all. The Mad Trapper of Rat River was a really tough guy, we feel pretty cocky having walked over his grave. As teenage girls will do, we still run and scream with pretended terror on our first pass over his 'peaceful' resting place.

In the morning a huge pot of porridge has replaced the huge pot of stinky stew, pretty gluey, but it is edible at least. Lumpy milk gives some texture to the glue. Powdered milk is all that is available in this tiny community; someone forgot to stir the 'milk' I think. A-hah, the can of strawberry jam is still on the table, we smother the oatmeal glue with strawberry jam and laugh through pink teeth. We have to return to Inuvik in disgrace, we came in third in a volleyball tournament that only had three teams competing, oh my, I am glad there were no more teams.

An announcement is made over the intercom at SHSS (this is a brand new school, it is high tech) that the arts department will be holding auditions for actors and dancers to perform in a traditional play that will be competing at the Arctic Winter Games in Whitehorse in March 1972. H-m-m, now this sounds a little more promising. I wonder what type of dancing…what type of play. Acting is not my forte, but I love dancing.

A strange collection of kids gathers after classes to get more information on the play. Everyone wants to get this over with; M.A.S.H will be on T.V. soon. Our art teacher explains that the script will be a more modern 'interpretation' of a traditional Inuit storey. In essence they are looking for 'psychedelic' actors and traditional drum dancers. My ears tweak at 'traditional drum dancers', this is something that I've had experience with. There are mostly white kids trying out for the play, I expect that most of them don't know one end of a drum from another, there could be hope for me yet, try out's will be next week, I am excited.

I show up at the dancing audition wearing a traditional 'fancy' Itiggi (parkie) made out of Tuktu (caribou) hide. This parka is made from raw tanned Caribou hide, so while most of the meat and fat have been scraped off, it has its own special smell. It was made to keep its owner warm in -50 F Arctic winters; indoors in a crowded room it is torture. I am determined to make the cut; I sweat it out in this hair coat.

Some of the girls moan as I approach the stage. It really is not fair, I show up with the ultimate costume and as long as I remain upright I will probably get the part. Even at this time, in Inuvik, these parkas are rare. The drums start and I begin to dance, I am fortunate to have had lots of experience with traditional drum dances. Your body follows the heartbeat of the drums; it is in your blood if you listen for it, it comes naturally. I have the part! I am to be one of the dancers; I will be going to Whitehorse for the Arctic Winter games!

It becomes apparent that few to none of the other white kids can drum dance, none of the native kids show up feeling that drum dancing will make them look square, it is too old fashioned.

I am surprised that these groovy kids can't follow the drums, it should come easy. I try to help some of the girls. They decide that rather than use the school kids as dancers; they will add credibility to the performance by asking the Mackenzie Delta Drum Dancers to do the dancing. Oh no, there goes my trip to Whitehorse! I am devastated, life if not fair!

A few of the professional dancers have been watching the auditions, some of the older women see me leave, 'no, no White Girl, we can fix this', they say. I can see their laughing eyes, what will they do to fix this? Nobody can fix this. 'Come, come with us.' 'You are a good dancer, nice parkie too.' (see I told you the parkie would work) We are behind the stage in the actors room, they are looking for something, they keep laughing quietly, little giggles and whispered Inuk words, what are they doing?

'Come, come sit.' I sit in a chair and they stand so I can't see what they are doing. Fingers rub something cool and slightly greasy on my face. The quiet laughter is gathering momentum as they cover my face, 'h-o-l-y, look at her eyes, they are s-o-o- bright. They can't contain themselves as they happily apply more of their 'fix', they break into belly laughs. 'Let her see.' 'Look!' They step back from the chair; I see a very brown face with extremely blue eyes starring back at me. It takes me a few minutes to realize that it is me!

They put my parkie back on me and walk me back to the stage. 'See teacher, she is brown now.' 'She will dance with us, no one will know.' They turn and walk away leaving me standing there. The teacher looks at me and shrugs a 'what choice do I have' look. Even better than I could ever dream of, I am going to Whitehorse and I will be dancing with the famous Mackenzie Delta Drum Dancers, once in awhile you get better than you ask for, Mashi, mashi cho.

P.S. The elders covered my face with brown shoe polish, it takes days to totally get it out of creases in my skin, they thought it was hilarious. I had to use it every time I performed with them. It never truly left my skin for months. For back issues of my stories you can go to links on my website www.thewhitegirl.ca

INUVIK

LET THE GAMES BEGIN

Arctic Winter Games 1972
(part 1 of 2)

A malformed head rolls and bumps across the stage. 'Invisible' strings jerk the paper mache' creation sideways, two amateur puppeteers begin a tug of war that threatens to rip the face of the moon to pieces. Or is this the head of sister sun? Maybe it is the moon, who is the brother to sister sun? We are all very confused by this storey line.

This is the 1970's; interpretations of art and literature hit new heights of awareness and abstract 'creativity'. I am quite frankly confused. Our theatrical group is getting its first insight into an interpretation of an Inuit Legend about Igaluk, the brother who is the moon and who is destined forever to chase his sister, the sun. Our drama director is very groovy and wants to produce a play that is 'far out'. I understand why the art director would prefer to do his own interpretation of this legend, I believe that the original version whispers of incest.

We will be travelling to the Arctic Winter Games in Whitehorse, Yukon Territory; it is a really big city! We will be participating in the Arts and Entertainment section of the competition; people will be coming from all over the north to participate in these games, so exciting!

The Arctic Winter Games will be held in March 1972, we only have two months to figure out what we are doing. Or more like, two short months to understand what this groovy drama director want us to do, he keeps changing the game plan and we are having difficulty translating his interpretation. He often asks us if we 'can dig it?' We are not sure.

I will be dancing with the Mackenzie Delta Drum dancers and am watching this rehearsal strictly out of curiosity. Our dancing part will be explained once they sort out the acting part. We are shadow dancers; we stand in the dark and then dance out of the darkness with drums and flashing fingers that add drama and effect to the play. It is tremendous fun; it will be great to see the whole play come together.

Living happily in the north through a polar winter requires social interaction and being mentally and physically active. Becoming 'bushed' is the effect of an under stimulated brain which results in a mental hangover. We spend our leisure time at Samuel Hearne Secondary School, the almost new high school in Inuvik, N.W.T.

Recent canned TV arrived beyond the Arctic Circle; this had been a distraction but quickly became predictable. For the first weeks we watched all four hours of canned entertainment every night. From Sesame Street five days a week, to The Beachcombers on Sunday.

M.A.S.H is still worth dashing home for and without a doubt you have to be home Sunday for the Beachcombers, but the rest of television is kinda' anti-social. You sit in front of the box and everyone says 'SH-H-h-h if you try to talk to them. We miss playing volleyball with our friends. TV is too much butt time. Can you imagine sitting, watching and listening to people that you don't know, for four whole hours a day? Such a waste of time! Well-l-l maybe for Hockey Night in Canada, but we can jump and yell for goals and shake our fists at penalties. So there is some action, but to sit and just stare at that box for hours on a regular basis is just so-o-o boring!

Adults have their own sources of entertainment. Curling is a huge Canadian past time and serious business in the north…as serious as you can be with a Curling Club named P.T.O.T.N. The translation to this abbreviation is directly, The Piss Tanks of the North. You have to be over 19 to participate; we have no idea what they do behind their secured doors on ice-covered rinks! The legal drinking age changed from 21 to 19 in the summer of 1970, but few high school students are old enough to participate. If anyone harbored thoughts of sneaking in, it is almost impossible. In a small community most everyone has an idea of how old your are and for sure they know your parents, don't even think about it!

Flying to the Yukon! We are actually on our way, almost. Twenty-eight kids are lying in the empty belly of a DC3, tucked in between the ribs of the plane. It is very cold; they have removed all of the seats to make more room for more kids, plus our chaperones. We have to bring sleeping bags on our trip to Whitehorse. This will be our bedding while we are there. We are all cocooned inside of our bags trying to stay warm. Something is wrong with our plane. They don't want to unload us, as this is a 'small problem, which should only take a minute' that was the word two hours ago.

'Food, we need food!' Hungry teenagers compete with hungry wolves both in appetite and aggression when stomachs growl. They realize that they have to feed us; it will be only a few more minutes until the plane is ready to fly, but it will be a few hours until we land in Whitehorse. We will then have to get to our accommodation and unpack our costumes or uniforms…we will never make it without food, NOW!

Puffs of frozen breath and the dim lights in the frosty plane interior are making vision difficult. Larger condensation clouds are created with the arrival of hot containers. Hot food, more than anyone expected. Steaming cups of hot chocolate run out before it gets half way to the back of the plane. 'Give me a sip, careful you're going to drop it on Ian's head!'

Frozen hands shake in the cold as the warm cups unleash tremors from stiff fingers. The cups are passed around until a little moan is heard from the unfortunate ones that catch only a drip. "More is coming, tap her cool you guys, everyone will get some!' We are a team, we are competing in all different venues, but we are a team, we represent Inuvik, we will share with our friends.

'Hey give Karla first dibbs on the hot chocolate, she missed out!' Fresh cups of steaming cocao arrive to enthusiastic yells from starving kids. Smells of fried chicken waft towards the back, we must be dreaming, where on earth did they get fried chicken? The Hudson Bay Company donated the chicken to the Peanut Butter Shake Shack and people volunteered to cook up enough chicken to feed 28 kids plus escorts.

Sitting wrapped up in a sleeping bag lying in the belly of a DC3 plane filled with most of my best friends, eating fried chicken, there is nothing better. Oh yeah, the engines rev up and sound like they are supposed to. Vibrating kids bounce around on the insides of a metal planes gut. Excited faces with chicken filled smiles beam back at each other, life if good. We are going to Whitehorse!

With a roar we have lift off, in a few hours we will be in the Capital City of the Yukon, Whitehorse to participate in the 1972 Arctic Winter Games! Talk to you about it in a couple of weeks, Mashi Cho.

INUVIK

ARCTIC WINTER GAMES

(part 2 of 2 Whitehorse 1972)

A rough and bumpy ride over the Richardson Mountains has deflated the Adrenalin rush that we all swear kept this DC 3 airplane afloat as it lumbered over that black ridge of rock. Twenty-eight of us, all under the age of 19 and over the age of 13 are participants in the 1972 Arctic Winter Games that are being held in Whitehorse, Yukon Territory. We are in the 'cheap' seats; actually there are no seats. All of the seats were removed to make room for more of us; the participants. We are lying in our sleeping bags in the planes belly, no sweat in the Arctic man.

We are all slightly frozen, some have been sick from the ' bucking bronco' effect of the up and down drafts that rode us high and dropped us low while crossing over that frozen range of Richardson rock. We all swore we felt the biggest bump when we crossed over the Arctic Circle and some figured that after we crossed the circle it would be a quick down hill glide into the southern city of Whitehorse, not so, we are impatient with this flight.

Suddenly down below us we see lights, lots and lots of little lights. Now we see lights on roads from cars and trucks. They are so little down there, little dinky toys! Look at how huge this city is, lights are everywhere. In Inuvik we have very few streetlights and no one except the Government employees leave their outside lights on, it costs too much for electric power. Government Employees don't have to pay their utility costs if they agree to come and work in the frozen isolated post communities of the far north. So who pays for that?

Bump, bump and the brakes screech us to a halt. All windows on the DC3 are frozen and frosted over with condensation, we can only see halos of lights at the entrance to the Whitehorse terminal, 28 teenagers produce a lot of hot air. Tired, with fingers and toes slow to move after a long cold flight, we struggle out of our sleeping bag cocoons. Will we morph into butterflies or will we sting like Bees? We are suspecting that these big city kids will kick our pants?

There is no way any of them can come close to beating us in the Northern games. Our team of Inuit and Dene athletes are awesome. Our figure skating girls are really nervous; Jill is having anxiety attacks, they know that they are weak in their division. I am a little cocky; all I have to do is dance. I am dancing with the impressive Mackenzie Delta Drum dancers and because of the 'creative interpretation' of the Inuit legend that we are presenting as a play, I could roll around on the floor and it could become part of the drama.

Blurry eyed and squinting we enter the warmth of the Whitehorse Terminal. We are greeted with clapping and whistling from a crowd almost as big as our hometown. We freeze in our tracks, we don't know what they are doing, it's a bit scary, we are not sure what we have done, or even what to do. Eyes wide open we look at each other, our Chaperones step forward and start to shake hands. 'Oh-h, they are welcoming us!' A chant begins to welcome us a representatives of Inuvik, NWT. How groovy is this!

Frozen fingers forgotten, we shake hands, our smiles tentative. The adrenalin pumps again in our veins, we are proud to be here, we will do our best for our town and our Territory, smiles break into wide-open grins. Into a bus we are hustled. First stop is the Rec Centre (this is now the Transportation Museum) for orientation and housing assignments. Back into the bus, too many of us for the amount of seats, no big deal.

Sitting on laps of friends we all start to sing, changing the lyrics, 'Nah, nah, nah, nah hey, hey, hey lets win!' The bus circles around a huge traffic circle at the top of Two Mile Hill, just for fun the bus driver re-circles the circle to yells of encouragement from his bus load of athletes. This is a first bus ride for most of us, for a few it is their first time in an enclosed motorized vehicle.

This traffic circle is magic, it chutes us out down Two Mile Hill, again we are amazed to see all of the lights, can you imagine a city this big, in our neighbourhood? Our bus grinds to a stop in front of the Whitehorse Inn; the neon white horse that prances forward to state its business is awesome! (you can see it still at the Whitehorse Museum) Why did we stop? There are streetlights at second and Main Street in downtown Whitehorse; h-o-l-y-y we ARE in a big city! We have no streetlights in Inuvik.

Crossing over the Yukon River Bridge into Riverdale, the driver points out F.H. Collins, this is where most of the games will take place. Figure skating competitions will be held in the Jim Light Memorial Arena on 4th Avenue beside the 4th Avenue Residence. Our final destination is Coudert Hall, a former hostel that housed kids from communities so that they could attend public school. As in the NWT, few communities offered classes in school beyond grade seven.

We are given our room assignments. Several members of our group live in hostels in Inuvik at either Grollier Hall or Stringer Hall. The kids from Stringer are impressed with the individual rooms that house 4 students each. In Stringer Hall the beds are in a large dormitory lined up in rows with absolutely no privacy. I can relate just a little, I have to share a very small bedroom with one of my brothers, sharing this space with 3 other girls is wonderful, I have no sisters. This feels like a giant sleep over.

Buses are scheduled for pick up and delivery so that athletes can get to their venues. We eat our meals in Coudert Hall; our drama performance will be done right in Coudert Hall as well. (Coudert Hall is no longer beside Christ the King Elementary School) As a group we follow our teams from competition to competition, we are the cheerleaders. Jill falls on the ice at Jim Light, it looks like she has hurt herself. We are so very proud when she smiles through tears and gets up to finish her program.

Of course our Boys from the deep Arctic are amazing. Their exercises in strength and agility have become legend. People now show up simply to watch them as performers rather than competitors. They do back kicks that bounce a tiny hand made fur seal skyward. Balancing on one hand throwing up a backward kick that targets a 'seal' the size of your cell phone is beautiful to watch, especially because they do it with out effort They bounce upright on legs of coiled muscle.

In this time dog sled racing is part of the Arctic Winter games, Paul Sheridan won this dog race with six dogs, plus the added weight of a newspaper reporter Lorraine Pound who reported for the "Ulu" a Winter Games paper. They finished the race well ahead of the competition. This is the ARCTIC winter games after all, there has to be dogs!

It's our turn to entertain. The stage is very high, I need to pay attention, as I am easily distracted, a fall to the floor would embarrass me forever! Brown shoe polish is applied to my face, 'sit White Girl, stop moving!' I am glad that this will be the end of the shoe polish cover up. I have to cover my white face to blend in with the rest of the Mackenzie Delta Drum dancers. Our play tells of an old Inuit legend of brother moon and sister sun. We dancers are the 'drama' within the 'drama'.

The malformed paper Mache' head of the moon has finished its appearance and has rolled around and off of the stage. With great theatrics, drums pound and we, in our costumes of full length, raw tanned caribou hide itigis (parkas) step out with dignity, presenting swaying accents of white caribou against dark caribou and flourishing hands accentuated with tufts of fur.

The crowd is hushed as the drums pound out heart beat rhythms, swishing hides of caribou sway to the beat, the hands of the dancers each take on a life of their own as they weave tales with fingers reaching towards the elusive brother moon. Mukluked feet stomp on the old wooden stage, stamping out an echo of the drums. I feel sick, there are so many people out there! The lights are blinding, thank god, I can only see part of the crowd, the heat in my itigi is overwhelming.

As sudden as it begins the drums stop and we swing down into a full bow and wait. There is no sound, oh, oh…we are in trouble, it is quiet out there, not what we were told to expect at all. Thunderous applause, foot stomping and whistles erupt from the audience. Actors and actresses run out to join us in the full bow, oh my they like us. This is so cool; they really are being too nice. We are presented with Gold Ulus.

Back in the bus we head for the airport and our silver steed, the DC3 that will fly us into the darkness of a winter night and home again to Inuvik. Our bus driver gives us one last merry-go-round the traffic circle. As one, our group breaks into song…Nah, nah, nah, nah, nah, nah nah nah, hey, hey, hey Good Bye… thank you Whitehorse, such a friendly city that welcomes all Northeners and celebrates them in their differences. We are 100% colourful and proud of it!

INUVIK

...AND THIS IS THE END, MY FRIEND

Row upon row of narrow, gun metal grey beds with white covers line the walls and fill any spare floor space in the long, long dormitory where the girls sleep. Commercial grade linoleum in battle-ship grey gleams with a waxy shine. The aisle that runs between the beds is a gauntlet. I hold my small bag of clothing tight to my chest for security. My eyes stare straight ahead wondering which of these beds will be mine. I make no eye contact with any of the girls; eye-to-eye contact is construed as aggression and challenge. My white skin is challenge enough.

I am so very alone. H-s-s-s, h-s-s-s, girls hiss as I walk by. I stand tall, trying to look bigger than my diminutive size, I stare directly ahead. It takes forever to walk to that small white island of sanctity, my new bed. Finally, I reach where I will sleep. It is close to the fire exit; I will be able to escape if I have to. This is a huge relief, I am small and I am fast. This is a good sign, the further into the dorm we walked the more claustrophobic I felt, it's a long way from my bed to the main entry of Stringer Hall.

This is 1972, I am staying in Stringer Hall, an Anglican hostel that is home to Eskimo kids while they attend public school in Inuvik, NWT. I have two strikes against me, I am white and I have been raised Catholic. I should not be here. Three of my brothers are also staying in Stringer Hall, I can only talk to them on the way to school. They are three, I am one, I am totally alone.

These girls in Stringer Hall come from Inuit communities that I have not lived in. I think longingly of my friends from Coppermine (Kugluktuk), they would be happy to see me. To these girls I am a damned 'townie', a white girl that has crossed over their one remaining boundary of privacy and entered onto the tiny island that they call their own. They have to contend with confrontation and conflict from the town kids, the military kids and a long-standing competition with Grollier Hall.

Grollier Hall is a Catholic hostel and Stringer Hall is Anglican. Indians are Catholic and Eskimos are Anglican. We called these places Hostels; they now refer to them as residential schools. The Hostels were not schools in this time, they provided housing for kids so they could attend public school. The tiny native communities did not have enough children to warrant separate classes and seldom went past the sixth grade. Some of the little kids were sent to the hostels by their parents because times were tough at home; there are too many kids and not enough food.

Inuvik was a rough town. We moved here from Kugluktuk just a few months ago and will be moving again. Fort Smith is about as south in the NWT as you can get. Fort Smith NWT is to be our destination in a few short months. I am not sorry to be leaving Inuvik; I am sorry to be in Stringer Hall. I have to survive the next two weeks until my parents return from finding us a new home in 'Smith'.

I sit on my bed and wait. Closer and closer they come. They don't know that I understand some Inuiktitut. (Eskimo Language) I could never master the annunciation but understand the conversation. Muttering that 'I am an evil white bitch, what in the hell is she doing here anyway?' they want to know. 'I have no right to be here', I agree wholeheartedly with them, I do not want them to know that I understand what they are saying.

Direct and in my face and finally in English, 'what chou you doin' here white bitch?' 'You should not be here, this is no place for white townies.' 'We gonna pound the shit out of you, you tell, we pound you more.' My back is pressed against the wall; I am surrounded by at least 20 Eskimo girls. They are tough, they are strong, I will go down fighting, my fire escape exit is cut off. If I inflict damage it may make it worse for me, or they may think twice next time, I see no point in lying down.

Closer and closer they shut me in. Some have started to hiss again. The hissing is terrifying. I have my fists up, I wait for the first blow, once the first fist is thrown they will 'dog pile' me. 'Hey, what are you doing to my friend?' Faces turn and fists slowly come down. 'What chou' mean yer' friend Rosemary?' 'Where you know this white townie from?' 'She is a good friend of my cousin in Kugluktuk, so she is a good friend of mine, leave her be.'

My eyes meet the eyes of Rosemary Kuptana. I cannot cry, but she knows my gratitude. She walks over and puts her arm around my shoulders. 'You will not pound her, she is my friend,' she repeats, in that instant she has my eternal gratitude (to this day). I have reprieve, I know the second that Rosemary is not around I will be attacked again, but for now I am OK. Rosemary takes my things and walks me over to her bed, ' you sleep beside me, its better.' I can only shake my head in agreement. I will cry quietly into my pillow in the dark of the night.

Crash, sharp noises smash and clash together in the night, metal bed frames collide with each other. Dogs are barking and running wild in the black of the night past the long rows of beds. The girl's dorm is in chaos. A red glow from the fire escape light becomes an escape beacon for someone other than me. Girls are screaming in the noise and confusion. Slam, the bar on the fire door is pushed hard and frosted air fills the long hall. An intoxicated Romeo has fled, his amour' dampened by the on-slaught of dogs and security.

Giggles break out, we all know whose boyfriend it is. She is crying, the police will throw him in jail. She will not be able to leave the hostel for months because of his indiscretion. This is the weekend. Passes to go to town to 'walk around' are high in demand. None of us has any money and there is no place to really go, but it is freedom.

Cigarettes are spayed with perfume and left to dry on the ledge above the beds. Girls smoke them to get 'high.' The smell of sweet, cheap perfume and tobacco smoke drying is horrible, lit up the cigarettes make my head spin, I want to throw up. This becomes a source of amusement, they blow the smoke in my face calling me a 'proudie' cause I won't smoke the crap. Hair spray is sprayed directly into mouths. A girl is held down while the other girls spray the lacquered poison past her clenched teeth. This terrifies me. So far they don't want to waste the 'precious' fluid on me.

Going to school is an escape from the hostel. I am looking forward to Monday when I can see my 'friends' again and pretend that life is normal. Things change quickly, 'why are you in the hostel?' 'So what are you, some white Kuggie?' (Derogatory slang for Eskimo) My Dene friends are all in Grollier and the division there is obvious as well. I am not allowed to visit friends after school; I have to go directly to the hostel unless I am involved in sports.

Where do I belong? My town friends are now calling me the 'white kuggie', I am living and sleeping in a room with Eskimo girls that don't want me there and make sure that I know it. I want to go home, but we are moving yet again, where is home exactly? I am told that my Siamese cat Sam has died; he froze into the ice under our house. Sam, who has been my constant friend and confidante through all of my travels has left forever, forever is how long I miss him.

I need to have a shower. The shower in Stringer Hall is a long cold room decorated in small square green tiles. Showerheads pop out of the frigid green wall at four-foot intervals. I am very shy, we are modest in my home, I have no sisters and am not used to being naked in front of anyone including myself. I have to have a shower.

I wait, everyone has gone off to the chapel (I am not required to attend because I am Catholic) and I seize my opportunity. Quickly I grab my things and run for the shower, I should have at least half an hour before my tormentors return to the dorm. Rosemary has kept them from beating the daylights out of me, but she can't stop the prejudice that flashes in dark eyes and spills like poison from their lips.

Even with the hot water full on, it is cold in this huge empty space. I stand shivering below the spray splattering out of the wall four feet above my head. Echoes in the room startle me, small noises cause me to start like a beaten dog. I have kicked over the shampoo bottle and it sounds like a wall is collapsing in this cold and vacuous space.

I stand facing the wall rinsing shampoo from my hair when I begin to feel it. The hair on my arms starts to rise. I feel sick to my stomach. Instinctively I cross my arms over my chest. My legs start to shake and I am embarrassed, shaking has overtaken the shivering and I feel like a puppet jerked about by a compulsive puppet master. I am totally vulnerable. With water streaming down my face I turn ever so slowly, 30 pairs of eyes stare at me. Some point fingers, the hissing begins and they laugh at my difference, I am most certainly…the White Girl.

P.S. Thank you, thank you. I am stunned at the support that I have received from Yukoners. I am considering a new series, you will be the first to know. In the meantime the Northern Journal is running the White Girl Series under Dawn Kostelnik, in their Opinion section (norj.ca). I invite you to participate in my website www.thewhitegirl.ca it has been amazing! XXXOOO

P.P.S. Mashi Cho, NO SWEAT IN THE ARCTIC EH!

Dawn, the White Girl

To most Canadians the North is a special place – unique from the rest of Canada, a mysterious and unknown land. That fascination is in part defined by Aboriginal culture that remains untouched in our great country's hinterland, in a state of becoming as "progress" finds its way ever deeper into the northern frontier.

Enter the observations of Dawn, the White Girl who grew up in the midst of it over two decades in the '60s and '70s. She shares with the rest of us experiences and images through the eye of a young girl raised in tiny, remote Aboriginal communities in the Mackenzie Valley.

Breathless, compelling, with amazing imagery, she draws us into a wondrous life that for her was ordinary, day-to-day, but is about as far removed from our modern, materialistic, cell phone addicted, urban lifestyle as one can get.

Thanks to Dawn we glimpse a tiny bit of life in the far North – communities where people cared for one another, out on the land, at one with nature – the way it once was.

Don Jaque, Publisher Northern Journal

11666521R00133

Made in the USA
San Bernardino, CA
24 May 2014